STAND OUT

Evidence-Based Learning for College and Career Readiness

THIRD EDITION

BASIC

WORKBOOK

ROB JENKINS

STACI JOHNSON

NATIONAL GEOGRAPHIC LEARNING | CENGAGE Learning·

Australia • Brazil • Mexico • Singapore • United Kingdom • United States

Stand Out Basic: Evidence-Based Learning for College and Career Readiness, Third Edition

Rob Jenkins and Staci Johnson

Workbook

Publisher: Sherrise Roehr

Executive Editor: Sarah Kenney

Development Editor: Lewis Thompson

Assistant Editor: Patricia Giunta

Director of Global Marketing: Ian Martin

Executive Marketing Manager: Ben Rivera

Product Marketing Manager: Dalia Bravo

Media Researcher: Leila Hishmeh

Director of Content and Media Production: Michael Burggren

Production Manager: Daisy Sosa

Senior Print Buyer: Mary Beth Hennebury

Cover and Interior Designer: Brenda Carmichael

Composition: Lumina

Main Image: Portra Images/Getty Images

Bottom Images: (Left to Right) Jay B Sauceda/ Getty Images; Tripod/Getty Images; Dear Blue/Getty Images; Portra Images/Getty Images; Mark Edward Atkinson/Tracey Lee/ Getty Images; Hero Images/Getty Images; Jade/Getty Images; Seth Joel/Getty Images; LWA/Larry Williams/Getty Images; Dimitri Otis/Getty Images

Work Book
ISBN 13: 978-1-305-65522-5

National Geographic Learning/Cengage Learning
20 Channel Center Street
Boston, MA 02210
USA

Cengage Learning is a leading provider of customized learning solutions with office locations around the globe, including Singapore, the United Kingdom, Australia, Mexico, Brazil and Japan. Locate our local office at: **international.cengage.com/region**

Cengage Learning products are represented in Canada by Nelson Education, Ltd.

Visit National Geographic Learning online at **NGL.Cengage.com**
Visit our corporate website at **www.cengage.com**

Printed in the United States of America
Print Number: 04   Print Year: 2018

CONTENTS

TO THE TEACHER

ABOUT THE SERIES

The **Stand Out** series is designed to facilitate *active* learning within life-skill settings that lead students to career and academic pathways. Each student book and its supplemental components in the six-level series expose students to competency areas most useful and essential for newcomers with careful treatment of level appropriate but challenging materials. Students grow academically by developing essential literacy and critical thinking skills that will help them find personal success in a changing and dynamic world.

STAND OUT WORKBOOK

The **Stand Out Workbook** is designed to provide additional practice for learners to reinforce what they learned in each student book lesson. It can be used as homework or a supplement to the lesson in the classroom. Each lesson in **Stand Out** is driven by a life-skill objective and supported by vocabulary and grammar. Students are not expected to master or acquire vocabulary and grammar completely after being exposed to it just one time, hence the need for additional practice. The lessons in the student book are three pages long and each supporting workbook lesson is also three pages long. The workbook lessons correlate directly with the student book lessons.

The **Stand Out Workbook** establishes a link to new content by providing the essential vocabulary introduced in the books often in a way that also promotes critical thinking skills. Promoting critical thinking skills is essential for students to become independent lifelong learners. About half of the three-page practice is grammar focused where students are given a chart with notes, study how the grammar facilitates communication, and gain additional needed confidence through practice.

HOW TO USE THE STAND OUT WORKBOOK

The workbook can be used in the following ways:

1. The activities in the workbook can be used as additional practice during the class to reinforce one or more practice activities in the student book.

2. The activities in the workbook can be assigned as homework. This is often a good way to reinforce what students have learned. The skills, vocabulary, and structures may not transfer into long-term memory after the lesson, so reinforcing the lesson after a short period of time away can be very helpful. Additionally, teachers can also review the homework at the beginning of each class, giving students another opportunity to be exposed to the information. Reviewing the homework is also a good strategy for the *Warm-up/Review* portion of the lesson and can be used in place of the one proposed in the **Stand Out Lesson Planner**.

3. The **Stand Out Workbook** can be used as a tool in the flipped classroom. In flipped classrooms, students prepare for lessons away from class before they are presented. Since the **Stand Out Workbook** introduces much of the vocabulary and grammar for each lesson, it is ideal for incorporating this approach.

ADDITIONAL PRACTICE

The **Stand Out** series is a comprehensive one-stop for all student needs. There is no need to look any further than the resources offered. Additional practice is available through the online workbook, which is different from the print workbook. There are also hundreds of multi-level worksheets available online. Please visit ngl.cengage.com/so3 to get easy access to all resources.

GOAL ■ Greet people

A. **Read.**

Hi!

Hello!

Welcome to our class.

How are you?

Fine! How are you?

B. **Write the greeting words and phrases from Exercise A.**

1. _____

2. _____

3. _____

4. _____

5. _____

C. Read the conversations.

Safa

Maria

Paulo

Hans

Safa: Hello, I am Safa.

Maria: Hi, I am Maria.

Safa: Nice to meet you, Maria.

Maria: Nice to meet you, too.

Paulo: Hi.

Hans: Hello.

Paulo: I am Paulo.

Hans: Nice to meet you. I am Hans.

D. Write a conversation.

Safa: Hello, I am Safa.

Hans: Hi, I *am* . . . _____.

Safa: _____

Hans: _____

E. Read the chart.

I am and I'm				
Greeting	Subject	Verb	Name	Example sentence
Hi	I	am	Hans	Hi, I am Hans.
Hello			Maria	Hello, I am Maria.
Greeting	Contraction		Name	Example sentence
Hi	I'm		Sylvia	Hi, I'm Sylvia.
Hello			Oscar	Hello, I'm Oscar.

F. Rewrite the sentences.

1. I am Silvia. _I'm Silvia._____

2. I am Oscar. _____

3. I am Ruby. _____

4. I am Orlando. _____

5. I am Taylor. _____

6. I am Satsuki. _____

G. Write a conversation with contractions.

         Duong   **Eva**

Duong: _Hello._____

Eva: _____

Duong: _____

Eva: _____

H. Circle the sentence(s) about you.

I'm a student.

I'm Maria.

I'm Fred.

I'm the teacher.

GOAL ■ Say and write phone numbers

A. Write the numbers over the words.

1		
one		six
2		
two		seven
three		eight
four		nine
five		ten

B. Copy the words.

one _____

two _____

three _____

four _____

five _____

six _____

seven _____

eight _____

nine _____

ten _____

C. Read the phone list.

Phone List	
Name	**Phone number**
Satsuki	(310) 555-1225
Ms. Adams	(619) 555-7843
Elsa	(714) 555-9856
Mirna	(562) 555-3534
Maria	(617) 555-7798
Orlando	(508) 555-4375

D. Write the phone number for each person.

1. Satsuki _____

2. Ms. Adams _____

3. Elsa _____

4. Mirna _____

5. Maria _____

6. Orlando _____

E. Read the chart.

I am and *It is (It's)*			
Subject	**Verb**	**Information**	**Example sentence**
I	am	Benjamin Paula	I am Benjamin. *(I'm Benjamin.)* I am Paula. *(I'm Paula.)*
The phone number	is	555-3456	The phone number is 555-3456.
It	is	555-3456	It is 555-3456. *(It's 555-3456.)*
My number	is	555-3456	My number is 555-3456.

F. Rewrite the sentences with *It's*.

Question:

What's your phone number?

Answers:

1. The number is 893-7234. It's 893-7234. _____

2. The number is 777-3245. _____

3. The number is 555-2235. _____

4. It is 327-8564. _____

5. It is 981-4392. _____

6. It is 972-2224. _____

7. The phone number is 283-9764. _____

8. The phone number is 765-2876. _____

G. Answer the questions about the phone list in Exercise C.

1. What is Satsuki's phone number? _____

2. What's Ms. Adams's phone number? _____

3. What's Elsa's number? _____

4. What's Mirna's phone number? _____

5. What is Maria's number? _____

6. What's Orlando's number? _____

H. Answer the questions.

1. What's your name? _____

2. What's your phone number? _____

GOAL ■ Follow instructions

A. Look at the words.

| teacher | answer | book | paper | word | name |

B. Write the words.

book

Amal

school

$3 + 2 = ⑤$

C. Circle *T* for true and *F* for false.

1. Listen to the teacher.   T   F

2. Read the student.   T   F

3. Circle the teacher.   T   F

4. Write your name.   T   F

D. Read the chart.

Action Verbs		
Action verb		**Example sentence**
read	a book	Read a book.
write	your name	Write your name.
listen	to the teacher	Listen to the teacher.
point	to the answer	Point to the answer.
repeat	the word	Repeat the word.
circle	the word	Circle the word.
check	the answer	Check the answer.

E. Look at the chart again and complete the sentences.

1. _____ a book.

2. _____ your name.

3. _____ to the teacher.

4. _____ to the answer.

5. _____ the word.

6. _____ the word.

7. _____ the answer.

F. Check (✓) the words that go together.

read

☐ a book

☐ a student

☐ the teacher

☐ the word

write

☐ a student

☐ the word

☐ your name

☐ the teacher

listen to

☐ the radio

☐ the teacher

☐ the student

☐ a book

check

☐ the answer

☐ a student

☐ a book

☐ a teacher

G. Complete the sentences. Use information from Exercise F.

1. Read _____.

2. Read _____.

3. Listen to _____.

4. Listen to _____.

5. Listen to _____.

6. Write _____.

7. Write _____.

8. Check _____.

H. Follow the classroom instructions.

1. Circle the answer.   3+2 =   5   10   1   0

2. Write your name.   _____

3. Repeat the word three times.   *pencil*

LESSON ① What's your name?

GOAL ■ Identify people

A. Read.

I'm Matías.
I'm a student.

I'm Irma.
I'm a student.

I'm Christine.
I'm a student.

I'm Binh.
I'm a student.

B. Complete the table.

Man	Woman	Student
Matías		

C. Read the table and complete the sentences.

Teachers	Students	Friends
Edgar	Maria	Maria and Ana
Tuba	Ana	Rudy and Casper
Ginger	Rudy	Lien, Ginger, and Tuba
Lien	Casper	Casper and Lien

1. Edgar is a _____.

2. Maria is a _____.

3. Ana and Rudy are _____.

4. Rudy and Casper are _____.

5. Ginger is a _____.

6. Lien, Ginger, and Tuba are _____.

7. Lien is a _____.

8. Maria and Ana are _____.

D. Read the paragraph and complete the class list.

Henry is a student in Hugo Matte's class. Henry is a good student. Ana is in the class, too. They are friends. Joseph is also a student. He has many friends. One of his friends is Marie. John, Albert, and Nika are in the class, too.

Class List for Hugo Matte	
	Name of student
1.	*Henry*
2.	
3.	
4.	
5.	
6.	
7.	

E. Make a list of students in your class on a separate piece of paper.

F. Read the chart.

Subject Pronouns			
Subject pronoun	**Verb**	**Information**	**Example sentence**
I	am	a student	I am a student. *(I'm a student.)*
You	are	the teacher	You are the teacher.
He		Roberto	He is Roberto.
She	is	Jasmin	She is Jasmin.
		a friend	She is a friend.
You		students	You are students.
We	are	teachers	We are teachers.
They		friends	They are friends.

G. Circle and write the correct word.

1. _____He_____ is a student.

(He)/ She / It

2. _____ is a student.

He / She / It

3. _____ are Joseph and Anna.

I / You / They

4. _____ am Amal.

I / You / We

5. _____ are Elsa and Hang.

I / You / We

6. _____ is a book.

He / She / It

H. Complete the sentences. Use pronouns.

1. Amal is a student. _____He_____ is from Egypt.

2. Elsa is a student. _____ is from Russia.

3. Amal and I are students. _____ are in the same class.

4. Mr. Jackson is a teacher. _____ is from Florida.

5. Mrs. Samuel and Mr. Jackson are from Florida. _____ are teachers.

I. Complete the sentences about you and another person in your class.

1. I am a student. _____ am from _____.

2. _____ is a student. _____ is from

_____.

LESSON **2** Where are you from?

GOAL ■ Express nationalities

A. Read the graph.

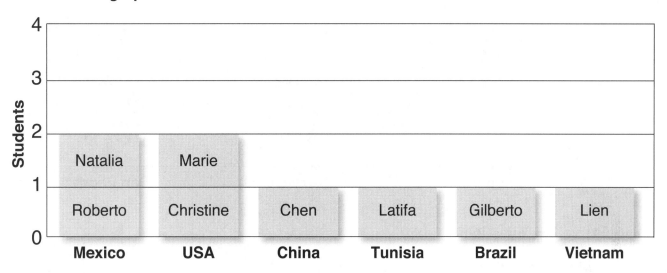

B. Write the countries.

1. Where are Marie and Christine from? _____

2. Where is Latifa from? _____

3. Where is Chen from? _____

4. Where is Lien from? _____

5. Where is Gilberto from? _____

6. Where are Roberto and Natalia from? _____

C. Read the story and complete the sentences.

> Mark is a teacher at Winchester Adult School. He is from the United States. Aiko, Nori, and Masa are students in his class. They are from Japan. Pablo and Guadalupe are students in his class, too. They are from Colombia.

1. Mark is from _____. He is a _____.

2. Aiko is a _____. She is from _____.

3. Pablo and Guadalupe are _____. They are from _____.

D. Read the graph.

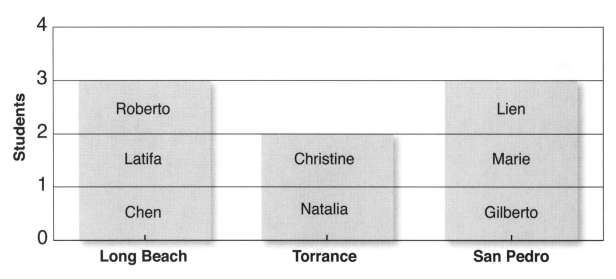

E. Answer the questions.

1. Where does Latifa live?   _____ *Long Beach* _____

2. Where does Natalia live?   _____

3. Where does Chen live?   _____

4. Where does Lien live?   _____

5. Where does Marie live?   _____

6. Where does Christine live?   _____

F. Read the chart.

Simple Present: *Live*			
Subject pronoun	**Verb**	**Information**	**Example sentence**
I	**live**	in Los Angeles in Chicago in Las Vegas	I live in Los Angeles.
You			You live in New York.
We			We live in Dallas.
They			They live in San Francisco.
He	**lives**		He lives in Chicago.
She			She lives in Las Vegas.

G. **Complete the sentences with *live* or *lives*.**

1. Chen _____lives_____ in Long Beach.

2. Natalia _____ in Torrance.

3. Roberto and Latifa _____ in Long Beach.

4. Lien, Marie, and Gilberto _____ in San Pedro.

5. Christine _____ in Torrance.

6. We _____ in Torrance.

7. I _____ in San Pedro.

8. You _____ in Long Beach.

9. The students _____ in Torrance.

10. Mr. Johnson _____ in Long Beach.

H. **Complete the sentences with *live* or *lives*.**

1. Juan is from Mexico. He _____lives_____ in Chicago.

2. Marie is from Haiti. She _____ in Tampa.

3. Josef and Anna are from Russia. They _____ in Tampa.

4. Gilberto and I are from Brazil. We _____ in Pasadena.

I. **Complete the sentences.**

EXAMPLE: _I am from Mexico. I live in Boston. Mike is from Portland. He lives in Oakland._

1. I am from _____. I _____ in _____.

Friends:

2. _____ is from _____.

_____ in _____.

3. _____ is from _____.

_____ in _____.

LESSON **3** **Are you married?**

GOAL ■ Express marital status

A. **Review the new words.**

| divorced | married | single |

B. **Match the pictures to the sentences. Draw a line.**

1.

Adem

a. They are divorced.

2.

Mirna and Paul

b. He is single.

3.

Laura and Jeff

c. They are married.

C. **Complete the sentences about the people in Exercise B.**

1. Adem is _____.

2. Mirna and Paul are _____.

3. Laura and Jeff are _____.

D. Read.

Martha is a good student. She is married and has two children. She is from the United States. She goes to Hastings Adult School.	**Alex and Marie** are married. They are from Russia. They are students at Hastings Adult School in Irvine.
Martin is my friend. He lives around the corner from the school. He is single. We go to school on Mondays and Wednesdays.	**María** is from Mexico. She comes to school every day. She is divorced.

E. Mark "X."

Name	Marital Status		
	Married	Single	Divorced
Martha	X		
Martin			
Alex and Marie			
María			

F. Read the chart.

The Verb *Be*			
Subject	*Be*	Marital status	Example sentence
I	am	married single divorced	I am married.
He She	is		He is single. She is divorced.
We You They	are		We are divorced. You are married. They are single.

G. Complete the sentences with the correct form of the verb *be*.

1. She ___is___ married.

2. They _____ divorced.

3. Enrique _____ divorced.

4. She _____ Maria.

5. We _____ single.

6. Duong and Lien _____ married.

7. Choi _____ from China.

8. You _____ students in my class.

9. Amal _____ single.

10. They _____ my friends.

11. We _____ from Brazil.

12. Oscar _____ a student.

13. Ms. Adams _____ a teacher.

14. I _____ from Chicago.

15. He _____ divorced.

16. They _____ married.

H. Write sentences about the students.

Name: Chen
From: China
Marital status:
Married

Name: Latifa
From: Saudi Arabia
Marital status:
Single

Name: Natalia
From: Guatemala
Marital status:
Divorced

Name: Christine
From: France
Marital status:
Single

1. Chen _is married_____. He _is from China_____.

2. Latifa _____. She _____.

3. Natalia _____. She _____.

4. Christine _____. She _____.

I. Write about you and a friend.

1. I _____. _____.

2. (a friend) _____. _____.

UNIT 1

L E S S O N **4** What's your address?

GOAL ■ Say and write addresses

A. Read the ID card and write.

LOCKE ADULT SCHOOL

First Name:	**Amal**
Last Name:	**Jahshan**
Street Address:	**8237 Augustin Street**
City:	**Irvine**
State:	**CA**
Zip:	**92602**

8883242442v

Name: _____

Address: _____

City: _____

State: _____

Zip code: _____

B. Complete the application for Amal Jahshan from Exercise A.

Jackson Adult School
PERSONAL INFORMATION
Name: Amal Jahshan _____
Street Address: _____
City: _____   State: _____   Zip Code: _____

C. Read the envelope.

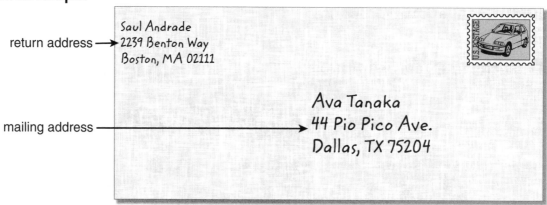

return address → Saul Andrade
2239 Benton Way
Boston, MA 02111

mailing address → Ava Tanaka
44 Pio Pico Ave.
Dallas, TX 75204

D. Complete the information.

Return Address

Name: Saul Andrade

Address: _____

City: _____

State abbreviation: _____

Zip code: _____

Mailing Address

Name: Ava Tanaka

Address: _____

City: _____

State abbreviation: _____

Zip code: _____

E. Read the chart.

The Verb *Be*			
Subject	***Be***	**Information**	**Example sentence**
I	**am**	a student	I am a student. (*I'm a student*)
He	**is**	a student	He is a student. (*He's a student.*)
She		a teacher	She is a teacher. (*She's a teacher.*)
it	**is**	265 Main Street	It is 265 Main Street. (*It's 265 Main Street.*)
the address		265 Main Street	The address is 265 Main Street.
the phone number		555-1234	The phone number is 555-1234. (*It's 555-1234.*)
Contraction		**Information**	**Example sentence**
I'm		a student	I'm a student.
He's		a student	He's a student.
It's		555-1234	It's 555-1234.
		265 Main Street	It's 265 Main Street.

F.   Write the sentences with contractions.

1. The address is 7734 Michel St.

   ___It's___ 7734 Michel St.

2. The phone number is 555-2376.

   _____ 555-2376.

3. He is a good student.

   _____ a good student.

4. I am from Haiti.

   _____ from Haiti.

5. The address is in the phone book.

   _____ in the phone book.

6. She is the teacher.

   _____ the teacher.

7. The phone number is 555-5672.

   _____ 555-5672.

8. I am happy here.

   _____ happy here.

9. I am married.

   _____ married.

10. She is from Brazil.

   _____ from Brazil.

G.   Write sentences about the mailing address in Exercise C.

The name _is Ava Tanaka_____.

The address _____.

The city _____.

The state _____.

The zip code _____.

H.   Complete an envelope from you (return address) to a friend (mailing address).

LESSON **5** What's your date of birth?

GOAL ■ Say and write dates

A. Write the year and read the calendar. _____

January	February	March	April	May	June

July	August	September	October	November	December

B. Write the dates from the calendar.

January 25th, _____	1-25-_____	1/25/_____

C. **Read the application form.**

Adult School Application			
Yamada	*Hanako*	*January 17th, 1962*	*Osaka, Japan*
Last Name	First Name	Date of Birth	Birthplace
2346 Wilbur Place	*Seattle*	*Washington*	*98103*	*(206) 555-1010*
Street Address	City	State	Zip Code	Phone

D. **Write the information.**

Address: _____

Birthplace: _____ Date of Birth:: _____

E. **Read the chart.**

What's and Contractions			
Questions			
Question word	**Verb**	**Information**	**Example sentence**
What	is	the date today your date of birth your birthplace your first name your last name your address	What is the date today? *(What's the date today?)* What is your date of birth? *(What's your date of birth?)* What is your birthplace? *(What's your birthplace?)* What is your first name? *(What's your first name?)* What is your last name? *(What's your last name?)* What is your address? *(What's your address?)*
Answers			
Subject	**Verb**	**Information**	**Example sentence**
The date today		September 1st, 2008	The date is September 1st, 2008. *(It's September 1st, 2008.)*
My date of birth		May 13th, 1965	My date of birth is May 13th, 1965. *(It's May 13th, 1965.)*
My birthplace	is	Mexico	My birthplace is Mexico. *(It's Mexico.)*
My first name		Maria	My first name is Maria. *(It's Maria.)*
My last name		Rodriguez	My last name is Rodriguez. *(It's Rodriguez.)*
My address		2341 First Street	My address is 2341 First St. *(It's 2341 First St.)*

F. Match the questions and answers.

1. What's your first name?
2. What's your phone number?
3. What's your birthplace?
4. What's your address?
5. What's your date of birth?
6. What's your zip code?

a. It's (562) 555-3534.
b. It's Buenos Aires, Argentina.
c. It's Robert.
d. It's 01275.
e. It's 3345 Gilbert Avenue.
f. It's June 1, 1965.

G. Write the questions.

Questions	Answers
What's your address?	It's 3344 South Main Street.
	It's Jon.
	It's July 2nd, 1975.
	It's 555-3737.

H. Complete the application form about yourself.

Adult School Application			
Last Name	First Name	Date of Birth	Birthplace
Street Address	City	State	Zip Code Phone

PRACTICE TEST

A. Look at the application form and circle the correct answers.

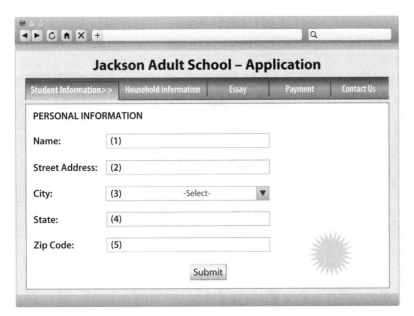

1. Where do you write *John Smith?*
   - a. (1)
   - b. (2)
   - c. (3)
   - d. (4)

2. Where do you write *92704?*
   - a. (1)
   - b. (3)
   - c. (4)
   - d. (5)

B. Look at the calendar and circle the correct answers.

1. What is the 2nd Tuesday?
   - a. 23rd
   - b. 11th
   - c. 9th
   - d. 18th

2. What day of the week is January 5th?
   - a. Monday
   - b. Friday
   - c. Saturday
   - d. Sunday

LESSON **1** Meet my friend

GOAL ■ Introduce yourself and others

A. Read the information.

Felipe
Student

Eva
Student

Gabriela
Teacher

Duong
Student

B. Complete the conversations.

Felipe: This is Gabriela. _She is the teacher_____.
Duong: Nice to meet you, Gabriela. _I'm Duong_____.
Gabriela: Nice to meet you, too.

Gabriela: I want to introduce Duong. _____.
Felipe: Nice to meet you, Duong. _____.
Duong: Nice to meet you, too.

Felipe: Meet Eva. _____.
Gabriela: Nice to meet you, Eva. _____.
Eva: Nice to meet you, too.

Duong: This is Eva and I am Duong. _____.
Felipe: Nice to meet you, Duong and Eva. _____.
Duong: Nice to meet you.
Eva: Yes, nice to meet you, too.

C. Practice the conversations.

D. Read the database.

First	Last	M/F	Address	City/State/Zip	Phone	DoB	Native country
Alberta	Ramos	F	23567 West Ave.	Palm, CA 92714	555-3321	07-02-1977	Mexico
John	Calvin	M	89456 Broadway	Palm, CA 92714	555-8934	02-25-1968	U.S.
Lien	Nguyen	F	33 Main St.	Palm, CA 92714	555-6734	06-27-1954	Vietnam
Duong	Nguyen	M	33 Main St.	Palm, CA 92714	555-6734	07-22-1955	Vietnam
Kenji	Nakamura	M	1298 Austin St.	Palm, CA 92714	555-1112	11-04-1970	Japan
Anya	Orlov	F	8264 Jackson St.	Palm, CA 92714	555-7564	09-13-1975	Russia

E. Answer the questions.

1. What's Alberta's address?

   Her address is _23567 West Avenue_____.

2. What's Kenji's last name?

   His last name is _____.

3. What's Anya's native country?

   Her native country is _____.

4. What's Lien's zip code?

   Her zip code is _____.

> **ABBREVIATIONS**
> Ave. = Avenue
> St. = Street
> DoB = Date of Birth

F. Read the chart.

Possessive Adjectives		
Pronoun	**Possessive adjective**	**Example sentence**
I	My	**My** phone number is 555-3456.
You	Your	**Your** address is 2359 Maple Drive.
He	His	**His** name is Edgar.
She	Her	**Her** name is Julie.
We	Our	**Our** last name is Perez.
They	Their	**Their** teacher is Mr. Jackson.

G. Complete the sentences with possessive adjectives.

1. ___Her___ phone number is 555-7564. (Anya)

2. _____ address is 1298 Austin Street. (Kenji)

3. _____ phone number is 555-6734. (Lien and Duong)

4. _____ native country is Australia. (you)

5. _____ last name is Ramos. (Alberta)

6. _____ last name is Nguyen. (Lien and Duong)

7. _____ birth date is February 25, 1968. (John)

8. _____ native country is Guatemala. (you and I)

H. Write sentences. Use the database in Exercise D.

1. Alberta is from Mexico. ___Her___ address is ___23567 West Avenue___.

2. John lives in Palm, California. _____ phone number is _____

3. Lien and Duong are married. _____ native country is _____

4. Anya and I are classmates. _____ teacher is Mrs. Jones.

5. I am from Russia. _____ teacher is _____

6. I am from Japan. _____ last name is _____

7. Duong and I live in Palm, California. _____ phone number is _____

8. We are students. _____ native countries are _____, Japan, and Vietnam.

9. I am John. _____ last name is _____

10. Anya is a student. _____ date of birth is _____

I. Complete the database with your information.

First	Last	Phone	Date of birth
Alberta	Ramos	555-3321	07-02-1957

LESSON **2** Where's the pencil sharpener?

GOAL ■ Describe your surroundings

A. Complete the words under the pictures.

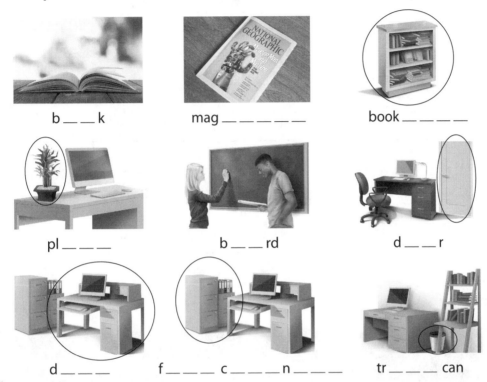

b _ _ k   mag _ _ _ _ _   book _ _ _ _ _

pl _ _ _ _   b _ _ rd   d _ _ r

d _ _ _ _   f _ _ _ c _ _ _ n _ _ _ _   tr _ _ _ _ can

B. Write the words in alphabetical order (a–z).

1. board

2. _____

3. _____

4. _____

5. _____

6. _____

7. _____

8. _____

9. _____

C. Complete the chart about your classroom.

Quantity (how many)	Object
1	board
	doors
	chairs

D. Read the chart.

Prepositions of Location		
Preposition		**Example sentence**
next to		The teacher is **next to** the door.
on		The book is **on** the desk.
in		The students are **in** the classroom.
between		The books are **between** the desk and the computers.
behind		The file cabinets are **behind** the computers.
in front of		The board is **in front of** the desk.

E. Look at the picture and check (✓) the correct answers.

1. on the desk

    ☐ the chair   ☐ the plant   ☐ the clock   ☐ the file cabinet

2. next to the pencil sharpener

    ☐ the computers   ☐ the chairs   ☐ the books   ☐ the pencil

3. on the wall

    ☐ the trash can   ☐ the plant   ☐ the clock   ☐ the desk

4. between the door and the board

    ☐ the clock   ☐ the students   ☐ the chairs   ☐ the computers

F. Complete the sentences about the picture.

1. The students are _____ the board.

2. The books are _____ the bookcase.

3. The file cabinets are _____ the computers.

4. The pencil sharpener is _____ the table.

G. Complete the sentences about your classroom.

1. The board is _____.

2. The trash can is _____.

3. The books are _____.

LESSON ❸ What are you doing?

GOAL ▪ Identify common activities

A. Complete the table with the words under the pictures.

a book

on a sheet of paper

a CD

in a notebook

music

a note

the teacher

a magazine

a friend

Listen to...	Talk to	Read	Write
the teacher			

B. Write sentences using the table in Exercise A.

1. I _listen to the teacher._

2. I _____

3. I _____

4. I _____

5. I _____

6. I _____

7. I _____

8. I _____

C. Complete the sentences with the words from the box. They can be used more than once.

is listening	is talking	is writing
is reading	is sitting	is standing

1. Marie is a student. She _____ in her notebook.

2. Gilberto is the teacher. He _____ a book.

3. Sini is in class. He _____ in a chair next to the bookshelf.

4. Christine _____ to her friend about the class.

5. Anya _____ to the radio.

6. Gilberto is the teacher. He _____ in front of the class.

7. Hans is a student. He _____ on a sheet of paper.

8. Eva _____ a magazine.

D. Read the chart.

Present Continuous		
Subject	**Verb**	**Example sentence**
He Juan Alexi Adolfo	is reading is writing is listening is sitting is standing is talking	He is reading a book. He is writing his name. Juan is listening to the teacher. Alexi is sitting in a chair. Adolfo is standing in front of the class. He is talking to a partner.
She Maria Cynthia Marlene	is reading is writing is listening is sitting is standing is talking	She is reading a book. She is writing her name. Maria is listening to the teacher. Cynthia is sitting in a chair. Marlene is standing in front of the class. She is talking to a partner.

E. Rewrite the sentences in the present continuous.

1. Mario reads a book.

   Mario is reading a book. _____

2. Eva sits in a chair.

   _____

3. Kenji writes on a sheet of paper.

   _____

4. John listens to a digital music player.

   _____

F. Complete the sentences.

1. The teacher _____ *is listening* _____ (listen) to the student.

2. Juan _____ (talk) to Maria.

3. Cynthia _____ (stand) in front of the class.

4. Adolfo _____ (write) a letter.

5. Marlene _____ (sit) in the back of the room.

6. She _____ (read) a book.

7. The teacher _____ (write) on the board.

8. He _____ (talk) to the class.

9. Jim _____ (listen) to music.

10. Eva _____ (talk) on the phone.

G. Complete the sentences with what people are doing.

1. The teacher is _____.

2. My friend _____.

3. A friend _____.

LESSON **4** When is English class?

GOAL ■ Plan a schedule

A. Read the schedule. Match the time.

8:30 a.m.	English class
1:00 p.m.	Lunch
3:00 p.m.	Pronunciation class
5:30 p.m.	Work

B. Answer questions about the schedule in Exercise A.

1. When is English class? _It's at 8:30 a.m._ _____

2. When is lunch? _____

3. When is pronunciation class? _____

4. When is work? _____

C. Write sentences under the clocks.

It's six thirty.

D. Complete your schedule. Write the times.

	Breakfast
	English class
	Lunch
	Dinner
	Bedtime

E. Read the chart.

When's, It's, and Contractions			
Questions			
Question word	**Verb**	**Information**	**Example sentence**
When	is	English class pronunciation class lunch work bedtime	When is English class? *(When's English class?)* When is pronunciation class? *(When's pronunciation class?)* When is lunch? *(When's lunch?)* When is work? *(When's work?)* When is bedtime? *(When's bedtime?)*
Answers			
Subject	**Verb**	**Information**	**Example sentence**
English class	is	at 5:00	English class is at 5:00. *(It's at 5:00.)*
Pronunciation class		at 3:00	Pronunciation class is at 3:00. *(It's at 3:00.)*
Lunch		at 12:00	Lunch is at 12:00. *(It's at 12:00.)*
Work		at 9:00	Work is at 9:00. *(It's at 9:00.)*
Bedtime		at 11:00	Bedtime is at 11:00. *(It's at 11:00.)*

F. Rewrite the sentences with contractions.

1. When is work? It is at 7:00 a.m.

   When's work? It's at 7:00 a.m.

2. When is dinner? It is at 6:00 p.m.

   _____

3. When is school? It is at 8:00 p.m.

   _____

4. When is breakfast? It is at 6:30 a.m.

   _____

5. When is lunch? It is at 12:30 p.m.

   _____

6. When is bedtime? It is at 10:30 p.m.

   _____

G. Answer the questions about Exercise A.

1. When's English class? _It's . . ._____

2. When's lunch? _____

3. When's pronunciation class? _____

4. When's work? _____

H. Guess your teacher's schedule. Discuss in your next class.

	Breakfast
	English class
	Lunch
	Bedtime

LESSON **5** It's cold today

GOAL ■ Plan for weather

A. Read the sentences and circle the clothes you need.

1. It's rainy in Panama.

2. It's snowy in Montana.

3. It's sunny in New Orleans.

4. It's hot in Japan.

B. Write the conversations with information from Exercise A.

Panama

Ruben: _How's the weather in Panama today?_

Jennifer: _It's rainy._

Montana

Jim: _____

Caitlin: _____

New Orleans

Jacque: _____

Alexi: _____

Japan

Pam: _____

Lewis: _____

C. Complete the chart with the words.

raincoat   sandals   coat   scarf

t-shirt   umbrella   sweater

Hot	Sunny	Cold	Rainy

D. Read the chart.

Simple Present: *Need*			
Subject pronoun	**Verb**	**Information**	**Example sentence**
I You We They	need	an umbrella a t-shirt sandals boots	I **need** an umbrella. You **need** a t-shirt. We **need** sandals. They **need** boots.
He She	needs		He **needs** an umbrella. She **needs** boots.

E. Complete the sentences with *need* or *needs*.

1. It's hot. I _____*need*_____ sandals.

2. It's rainy. You _____ an umbrella.

3. It's cold. They _____ sweaters.

4. It's snowy. He _____ boots.

5. It's cold. She _____ a sweater.

6. It's hot. Ron _____ sandals.

7. It's rainy. We _____ raincoats.

8. It's hot. He _____ a t-shirt.

F. Circle *need* or *needs*.

1. It's rainy and cold. Maria _____ a sweater and an umbrella.	need	(needs)
2. It's windy and cold. Evelyn _____ a coat and a scarf.	need	needs
3. It's hot. Jim, Jenny, and Paul _____ warm clothing.	need	needs
4. It's snowy today. We _____ boots and gloves.	need	needs
5. It's cold. Jerry and I _____ coats.	need	needs
6. It's foggy and cold. They _____ sweaters.	need	needs
7. It's sunny. Kenji _____ a t-shirt.	need	needs
8. It's hot and sunny. You _____ sandals.	need	needs

G. Complete the paragraph with *need* or *needs*.

Martha is a student at Oak Haven Adult School. She goes to school in the morning. It is cold most mornings. She _____ a sweater every morning. Today, it's rainy. She _____ an umbrella. Her friends live in Mexico. It's hot most days. They _____ t-shirts and sandals most days.

PRACTICE TEST

A. Look at the pictures and circle the correct answers.

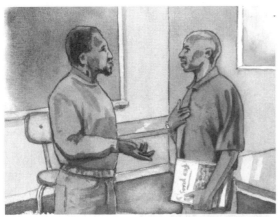

1. What are they doing?
   a. They are talking in the classroom.
   b. They are reading a book.
   c. They are writing.
   d. They are listening to the teacher.

2. What is she doing?
   a. She is talking.
   b. She is listening.
   c. She is writing.
   d. She is standing.

B. Look at Milly's schedule and circle the correct answers.

Milly's Schedule	
8:00 a.m.	Read a book
10:00 a.m.	English class
12:00 p.m.	Lunch
2:00 p.m.	Work

1. When does Milly eat?
   a. at 8:00 a.m.   b. at 10:00 a.m.
   c. at 12:00 p.m.   d. at 2:00 p.m.

2. When does Milly practice English?
   a. at 8:00 a.m.   b. at 10:00 a.m.
   c. at 12:00 p.m.   d. at 2:00 p.m.

LESSON **1** Let's eat!

GOAL ■ Identify common foods

A. Match the foods with the pictures. Draw lines.

sandwich

apple

eggs

tomato

banana

B. Unscramble the words from Exercise A.

1. motato   <u>   tomato   </u>

2. nabaan   <u>   </u>

3. sgeg   <u>   </u>

4. dwisahnc   <u>   </u>

5. palep   <u>   </u>

C. Write the words in the correct shopping list.

apples	tuna	milk	potatoes	turkey
bananas	chicken	oranges	tomatoes	water

	Meat/Fish

	Fruits/Vegetables

	Drinks

D. Add other words to the lists in Exercise C.

E. Read the chart.

Prepositions of Location		
Preposition		**Example sentence**
in		The tuna fish is **in** the canned goods section.
on		The green beans are **on** the top shelf.
over		The corn is **over** the tomato sauce.
between		The tomato sauce is **between** the pears and the tuna fish.
next to		The peas are **next to** the corn.

F. Complete the sentences about the picture.

1. The corn is over the _____ *tomato sauce* _____.

2. The tuna fish is next to the _____.

3. The corn is between the _____ and the _____.

4. The green beans are over the _____.

5. The green beans are next to the _____.

6. The tomato sauce is between the _____ and the _____.

G. Complete the conversations about the picture in Exercise F.

Customer: Where are the peas?
Salesperson: The peas are _*next to the corn*_____.

Customer: Where are the pears?
Salesperson: The pears are _____.

Customer: Where is the corn?
Salesperson: The corn is _____.

Customer: Where is the tuna?
Salesperson: The tuna is _____.

Customer: Where is the tomato sauce?
Salesperson: The tomato sauce is _____.

Customer: Where are the green beans?
Salesperson: The green beans are _____.

LESSON 2 I'm hungry

GOAL ■ Express hunger

A. Look at the meals for lunch and dinner.

chicken sandwich

tuna fish sandwich

rice and vegetables

hamburger and fries

tacos

spaghetti

B. Which meals do you like in Exercise A?

1. My favorite is _____.

2. Next, I like _____.

3. Next, I like _____.

C. Make a list of your favorite meals.

1. _____

2. _____

3. _____

4. _____

5. _____

D. Write your breakfast, lunch, and dinner for today.

Breakfast	Lunch	Dinner

E. Read the chart.

Simple Present: *Be*			
Affirmative *(yes)*			
Subject	***Be***	**Information**	**Example sentence**
I	am	hungry very hungry thirsty	I **am** hungry. (*I'm hungry.*)
He She	is		He **is** hungry. (*He's hungry.*)
			She **is** hungry. (*She's hungry.*)
We You They	are		We **are** hungry. (*We're hungry.*)
			You **are** hungry. (*You're hungry.*)
			They **are** hungry. (*They're hungry.*)
Negative *(no)*			
Subject	***Be***	**Information**	**Example sentence**
I	am not	hungry very hungry thirsty	I **am not** hungry. (*I'm not hungry.*)
He She	is not		He **is not** hungry. (*He's not hungry.*)
			She **is not** hungry. (*She's not hungry.*)
We You They	are not		We **are not** hungry. (*We're not hungry.*)
			You **are not** hungry. (*You're not hungry.*)
			They **are not** hungry. (*They're not hungry.*)

F. **Complete the sentences with the affirmative (yes) verb *be*.**

1. John and Marie _____*are*_____ hungry.   2. I _____ thirsty.

3. We _____ very hungry.   4. The students _____ very thirsty.

5. Tuba _____ hungry.   6. Abraham and I _____ hungry.

7. You _____ very hungry.   8. They _____ very thirsty.

9. She _____ hungry.   10. He _____ thirsty.

11. Mario _____ hungry.   12. The teacher _____ hungry.

G. **Rewrite Exercise F with the negative (no) verb *be*.**

1. John and Marie _____*are not*_____ hungry.

2. I _____ thirsty.

3. We _____ very hungry.

4. The students _____ very thirsty.

5. Tuba _____ hungry.

6. Abraham and I _____ hungry.

7. You _____ very hungry.

8. They _____ very hungry.

9. She _____ hungry.

10. He _____ thirsty.

11. Mario _____ hungry.

12. The teacher _____ hungry.

LESSON **3** Let's have spaghetti

GOAL ■ Plan meals

A. Look at the words.

| jar | package | can | bag | pound |

B. Write the word under each picture.

b _____   c _____   j _____

pa _____   po _____

C. Read the paragraph and underline the containers.

Keiko needs a few things from the store for her camping trip. She needs three cans of beans and two bags of potato chips. She also wants a jar of her favorite food—peanut butter.

D. Complete the sentences about the paragraph.

Keiko needs three cans of _____.

Keiko needs two bags of _____.

Keiko wants one jar of _____.

E. Read the chart.

Singular and Plural			
Regular		**Exceptions**	
Singular	**Plural**	**Singular**	**Plural**
jar	jars	potato	potato<u>es</u>
can	cans	tomato	tomato<u>es</u>
bag	bags	sandwich	sandwich<u>es</u>
pound	pounds		
carrot	carrots		
apple	apples		
egg	eggs		

F. Write the plurals.

1. apple _____ apples _____

2. sandwich _____

3. tomato _____

4. jar _____

5. bag _____

6. onion _____

7. egg _____

8. bottle _____

9. box _____

10. package _____

11. radish _____

12. potato _____

G. Complete the sentences about the pictures.

1.
2.

3.
4.

1. We need two _____ eggs _____ and one _____ .

2. I need three _____ and one _____ .

3. We need one _____ and one _____ .

4. We need one _____ and two _____ .

H. Complete the shopping list.

	Shopping List	
2 _____ of tomato sauce	3 eg _____
1 _____ of spaghetti	4 pot _____
5 _____ of ground beef	6 ban _____

I. Complete the paragraph.

I want to make spaghetti for dinner. I need two _____ of tomato sauce, one _____ of spaghetti, and five _____ of ground beef. I also need a few other things from the store. I need three _____, four _____, and six _____ .

LESSON 4 What's for dinner?

GOAL ■ Make a shopping list

A. Read the Venn diagram about Lien and Molly's shopping lists.

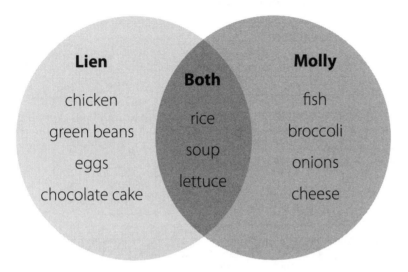

Lien

chicken

green beans

eggs

chocolate cake

Both

rice

soup

lettuce

Molly

fish

broccoli

onions

cheese

B. Complete the shopping lists for Lien and Molly.

Lien	Molly

C. Read the shopping list.

Shopping List		
milk	chicken	green beans
turkey	tuna	carrots
eggs	broccoli	
yogurt	oranges	
bananas	pears	

D. Write the foods from Exercise C in the table.

Meat/Fish	Vegetables	Fruit	Dairy
			milk

E. Read the chart.

Simple Present *Want*			
Subject	Verb	Information	Example sentence
I You We They	want	apples water milk carrots cheese tomatoes	I **want** apples. You **want** water. We **want** milk. They **want** carrots.
He She	wants		He **wants** cheese. (Amadeo wants cheese.) She **wants** tomatoes. (Lidia wants tomatoes.)

F. Circle the correct word.

1. Edgar and Akisha _____ sandwiches.   (want)   wants

2. I _____ bananas and oranges.   want   wants

3. Sally _____ broccoli and lettuce.   want   wants

4. We _____ milk and yogurt.   want   wants

5. They _____ tomatoes and lettuce.   want   wants

6. Martin _____ cheese.   want   wants

7. She _____ a tomato sandwich.   want   wants

8. You _____ a hamburger and fries.   want   wants

9. The brothers _____ breakfast.   want   wants

10. Ingrid _____ carrots.   want   wants

G. Complete the sentences with *want* or *wants*.

1. Amadeo _____ apples, water, tomatoes, and chips.

2. Marta _____ oranges, apples, and bananas.

3. Marta and Amadeo _____ chicken.

4. Mario and I _____ lunch.

5. Jack _____ milk.

6. I _____ broccoli, lettuce, and tomatoes.

H. On a separate piece of paper, make a shopping list for a party. What food do you want at your party?

LESSON **5** What do you like?

GOAL ■ Express preferences

A. Look at the pictures.

B. Complete the table with the foods in Exercise A.

I like . . .	I don't like . . .

C. Write sentences about what you like from Exercise B.

Example: I like yogurt.

1. _____

2. _____

3. _____

4. _____

D. Write sentences using the information.

Name	likes . . .	eats . . .
Saul	chocolate cake	
Amadeo		pie
Yoshi		yogurt
Chen	fruit	
Rhonda	cookies	
Sue		ice cream

1. *Saul likes chocolate cake.* _____

2. _____

3. _____

4. _____

5. _____

6. _____

E. Read the chart.

Simple Present (Regular)			
Subject	Verb	Information	Example sentence
I You We They	like eat want need	ice cream cookies fruit vegetables cake	I **like** ice cream. You **eat** cookies. We **want** fruit. They **need** vegetables.
He She	likes eats wants needs		He **eats** cake. She **wants** fruit.

F. Circle the correct word.

1. Tien and Gregorio ((like) / likes) pizza and soda.

2. They (eat / eats) lunch at 12:00 p.m.

3. We (need / needs) cake for dessert.

4. He (like / likes) fruit for dessert.

5. Margaret and Rob (need / needs) potatoes.

6. Lidia (eat / eats) cookies for snacks.

7. You (want / wants) vegetables with your sandwich.

8. The teacher (like / likes) chocolate.

9. The students (need / needs) dessert.

G. Complete the sentences.

1. Kenji _____ (need) food for lunch.

2. Melissa _____ (want) dessert.

3. Jose and I _____ (like) pizza.

4. We _____ (eat) breakfast at 8:00 a.m.

5. You _____ (want) eggs.

6. I _____ (like) bananas.

7. She _____ (eat) dessert.

8. The students _____ (need) dinner.

H. Answer the questions.

1. What do you eat for lunch? _I eat . . . _____.

2. What do you like for breakfast? _____

3. What do you want for dinner? _____

4. What does your friend eat for lunch? _He/She eats . . . _____.

5. What does your friend like for breakfast? _____

6. What does your friend want for dinner? _____

PRACTICE TEST

A. Read and circle the correct answers.

> Nathan needs to go to the supermarket. He needs bananas, apples, and oranges. He needs carrots and strawberries, too. Nathan also wants to buy his favorite food: cheese!

1. What vegetable does Nathan need?

   a. He needs bananas.   b. He needs carrots.

   c. He needs apples.   d. He needs to go to the supermarket.

2. What is Nathan's favorite food?

   a. bananas   b. potatoes

   c. cheese   d. shopping

B. Read and circle the correct answers.

1. What time is breakfast?

   a. at 6:00 p.m.   b. at 7:00 a.m.

   c. at 7:00 p.m.   d. at 12:00 p.m.

2. What time is lunch?

   a. at 6:00 p.m.   b. at 6:00 a.m.

   c. at 12:00 p.m.   d. at 12:00 a.m.

LESSON ❶ What's on sale?

GOAL ■ Identify types of clothing

A. Write the words from the box next to the clothing.

baseball cap	scarf	t-shirt	gloves	shorts
coat	sweater	boots	sandals	sunglasses

B. Complete the table with the words from Exercise A.

Winter clothing	Summer clothing

C. **Write sentences about Lien's and Steve's clothing in Exercise A.**

1. Lien has a _scarf_____.

2. She has a _____.

3. She has _____.

4. She has a _____.

5. She has _____.

6. Steve has a _baseball cap_____.

7. He has a _____.

8. He has _____.

9. He has _____.

10. He has _____.

D. **Read the chart.**

Simple Present: *Have*			
Subject	**Verb**	**Information**	**Example sentence**
I You We They	have	a shirt *or* shirts a dress *or* dresses a blouse *or* blouses a sweater *or* sweaters a coat *or* coats	I **have** a shirt.
			You **have** three dresses.
			We **have** five blouses.
			They **have** sweaters.
He She	has		He **has** a coat.
			She **has** three blouses.

E. Circle the correct word.

1. She _____ three blouses and two pairs of pants.   have   (has)

2. They _____ red coats and red blouses.   have   has

3. The teacher _____ three pairs of shoes.   have   has

4. The students _____ white pants.   have   has

5. I _____ a brown pair of pants and brown socks.   have   has

6. We _____ blouses on sale for $32.00.   have   has

7. Maria and Lidia _____ shoes in their closets.   have   has

8. You _____ my coat.   have   has

F. Review the simple present tense. Read the chart.

Simple Present			
Subject	Verb	Information	Example sentence
I You We They	want need	a t-shirt a blouse a jacket shorts shoes	I want a t-shirt. You need a blouse. We want shorts. They need a jacket.
He She	wants needs		He wants shoes. She needs a blouse.

G. Complete the sentences.

1. I _____ (need) pants and a sweater.

2. They _____ (want) new blouses.

3. We _____ (have) blue shirts in our closets.

4. She _____ (have) a pair of red shorts.

5. Lien and Puc _____ (need) new clothes.

6. John _____ (have) a pair of black shoes.

7. They _____ (have) four shirts and three pairs of pants.

8. You _____ (have) five pairs of shoes in your closet.

LESSON ❷ Where's the fitting room?

GOAL ■ Ask for and give directions in a store

A. Look at the picture and write the letters from the box.

a. women's dresses	b. women's blouses	c. men's caps
d. children's socks	e. teen's pants	f. teen's dresses
g. children's pajamas	h. women's shoes	i. men's t-shirts

B. Write the section.

1. I want a dress for my mother. _____ Women's _____

2. He wants pants. _____

3. I need a blouse. _____

4. My children need clothes. _____

5. My son is 13 years old. He needs a shirt. _____

6. My daughter is 17. She needs a sweater. _____

C. Write sentences about Exercise B.

1. The dresses are _in the women's section_ _____.

2. The pants are _____.

3. The blouses are _____.

4. The clothes for children are _____.

5. The shirts for boys are _____.

6. The sweaters for girls are _____.

D. Read the chart.

Prepositions	
a. It's **in the front of** the store.	
b. It's **in the corner of** the store.	
c. It's **in the middle of** the store.	
d. It's **in the back of** the store.	
e. It's **on the left side of** the store.	
f. It's **on the right side of** the store.	

E. Look at the picture and complete the sentences.

1. The coats are _____.

    a. in the corner   b. in the middle   c. on the right side

2. The pants are _____.

    a. in the corner   b. in the middle   c. on the left side

3. The skirts are _____.

    a. in the corner   b. in the back   c. on the left side

4. The dresses are _____.

    a. in the corner   b. in the back   c. on the right side

F. Describe your classroom.

1. What is on the right side of the room? _____

2. What is on the left side of the room? _____

3. What is in the back of the room? _____

4. What's in the front of the room? _____

5. What's in the middle of the room? _____

6. What's in the corner of the room? _____

LESSON 3 What colors do you like?

GOAL ■ Describe clothing

A. Read the inventory.

Adel's Inventory List		
Quantity (How many?)	Item	Color
10	shirt	blue and green
15	blouse	white and yellow
8	sweater	red and blue
7	coat	black
1	dress	green
1	dress	red
2	dress	black

B. Answer the questions. Write numbers as words.

1. How many shirts are there? _____ ten _____

2. What colors are the sweaters? _____

3. How many blouses are there? _____

4. What color are the coats? _____

5. How many coats are there? _____

6. How many sweaters are there? _____

7. What colors are the dresses? _____

8. What colors are the blouses? _____

9. How many dresses are there? _____

10. What colors are the shirts? _____

C. Read.

Leti: I want a dress.
Salesperson: What color do you like?
Leti: I like yellow.
Salesperson: OK! What size?
Leti: Size 8, please.

Gaspar: I need a shirt.
Salesperson: What color do you like?
Gaspar: I like green.
Salesperson: Nice color! What size?
Gaspar: Medium, please.

Pedro: I a need sweater.
Salesperson: What color do you like?
Pedro: I like blue.
Salesperson: Great! What size?
Pedro: Small is good.

D. Complete the table.

Name	Item	Size	Color
Leti			
Gaspar			
Pedro			

E. Read the chart.

There is, There are	
Singular *(is)*	**Plural *(are)***
There **is** one green shirt.	There **are** two black shirts.
There **is** one pair of red shoes.	There **are** two pairs of shoes.
There **is** one blouse in the store.	There **are** three blouses in the store.

F. Answer the questions about Exercise A.

1. How many shirts are there? ___There are___ _____ ten shirts.

2. How many blouses are there? _____ fifteen blouses.

3. How many red dresses are there? _____ one red dress.

4. How many coats are there? _____ seven coats.

5. How many green dresses are there? _____ one green dress.

6. How many sweaters are there? _____ eight sweaters.

G. Write sentences about the inventory.

Adel's Inventory List		
Quantity	Item	Size
3	shirt	small
2	shirt	medium
1	shirt	large
2	shirt	extra large

1. How many small shirts are there?

   ___There are three small shirts._____

2. How many medium shirts are there?

   _____

3. How many large shirts are there?

   _____

H. Write sentences about what is in your closet.

There are _____ in my closet.

_____

_____

LESSON **4** **That's $5.00**

GOAL ◼ Make purchases

A. Write the totals on the receipts.

1.
Adel's Clothing

shorts 15.50
t-shirts 12.75

TOTAL .... ⟨ 28.25 ⟩

2.
Adel's Clothing

blouse 18.00
dress 27.50
scarf 14.00

TOTAL .... _____

3.
Adel's Clothing

shirt 19.00
shoes 43.50

TOTAL .... _____

4.
Adel's Clothing

boots 22.25
coat 65.50

TOTAL .... _____

5.
Adel's Clothing

blouse 15.50
blouse 18.00

TOTAL .... _____

6.
Adel's Clothing

pants 19.00
shoes 22.50

TOTAL .... _____

B. What money do you need for the totals in Exercise A?

	Total	$20 bills	$10 bills	$5 bills	$1 bills	Quarters
1.	28.25	1		1	3	1
2.						
3.						
4.						
5.						
6.						

C. Read the ad.

All Sizes

Save $5.00

$22.50

SALE

$33.00

All Sizes

SALE

All Sizes

$28.00

Adel's
CLOTHING EMOPORIUM

D. Answer the questions.

1. How much are the pants? $_____

2. How much is the shirt? $_____

3. How much is the sweater? $_____

E. Read the chart.

Simple Present: *is, are*			
Questions			
Question word	Verb	Information	Example sentence
How much	is	the blouse	How much is the blouse?
	are	the blouses	How much are the blouses?
Answers			
Subject	Verb	Information	Example sentence
the blouse (it)	is	$22.00	The blouse is $22.00. *(It's $22.00.)*
the blouses (they)	are	$20.00	The blouses are $20.00. *(They're $20.00.)*

F. Complete the sentences.

1. How much _____are_____ the sweaters? The sweaters _____are_____ $45.00.

2. How much _____ the blouse? The blouse _____ $22.00.

3. How much _____ the shoes? The shoes _____ $30.00.

4. How much _____ the dress? The dress _____ $55.00.

5. How much _____ the shirt? The shirt _____ $15.00.

6. How much _____ the shorts? The shorts _____ $13.00.

G. Put the words in the table.

blouse	shirt	shoes	sweater
dress	shirts	shorts	sweaters

How much is . . . ?	*How much are . . . ?*

H. Write questions using the information in Exercise G.

1. How much is the blouse? _____

2. _____

3. _____

4. _____

5. _____

6. _____

7. _____

8. _____

LESSON **5** How much are the shoes?

GOAL ■ Read advertisements

A. Look at the advertisement.

B. Answer the questions.

1. How much is the dress? _$33._

2. How much is the hat? _____

3. How much is the suit? _____

4. How much is the coat? _____

5. How much are the socks? _____

6. How much is the skirt? _____

7. How much is the cap? _____

8. How much is the t-shirt? _____

9. How much is the sweater? _____

10. How much is the blouse? _____

C. Read the paragraph and answer the questions.

> My name is Marcus. I'm going on a trip with my friends. I need new clothes. I need four new shirts. I also need a pair of boots for walking. I need two pairs of blue jeans and heavy socks, too. This will be a great vacation!

1. How many shirts does he need? _____

2. How many pairs of boots does he need? _____

3. How many pairs of blue jeans does he need? _____

4. How many pairs of socks does he need? _____

D. Read the chart.

How much and How many				
Questions				
Question word		**Verb**	**Information**	**Example sentence**
How much	(money)	is	the blouse	How much is the blouse?
		are	the blouses	How much are the blouses?
Question word		**Question structure**		**Example sentence**
How many	blouses	do you want		How many blouses do you want?
Answers				
Subject	**Verb**	**Information**	**Example sentence**	
the blouse	is	$22.00	The blouse is $22.00. (It's $22.00.)	
the blouses	are	$20.00	The blouses are $20.00. (They're $20.00.)	
I	want	three blouses	I want three blouses.	

E.   Check (✓) the correct answer.

1. _____ are the shirts?   ☐ How much   ☐ How many

2. _____ is the blouse?   ☐ How much   ☐ How many

3. _____ dresses do you want?   ☐ How much   ☐ How many

4. _____ are the shoes?   ☐ How much   ☐ How many

5. _____ shirts do you want?   ☐ How much   ☐ How many

6. _____ sweaters do you want?   ☐ How much   ☐ How many

F.   Read the price list and circle the correct answer.

Adel's Price List		
Quantity	Item	Price
10	shirt	$27.00
2	shoes	$30.00
5	pants	$32.00
8	blouse	$22.00

1. How much are the blouses?

   a. 8   b. $22.00   c. item

2. How many pairs of pants are there?

   a. 5   b. $27.00   c. $32.00

3. How many shirts are there?

   a. $27.00   b. quantity   c. 10

4. How much are the shirts?

   a. $27.00   b. price   c. 10

5. How many blouses do they have?

   a. 8   b. shirts   c. $22.00

6. How much are the shoes?

   a. 8   b. 2   c. $30.00

PRACTICE TEST

A. Read the receipts and circle the correct answers.

Adel's Clothing	Boutique Chic	Clothes Warehouse
shorts $15.50	blouse $18.00	shirts $19.00
t-shirts $10.75	dress $27.50	shoes $28.25
	scarves $7.00	
Total $26.25	Total $52.50	Total $47.25
Customer Copy	Customer Copy	Customer Copy

1. How much is the blouse?

   a. $18.00   b. $19.00

   c. Adel's Clothing   d. Total

2. Where do you buy shorts?

   a. Boutique Chic   b. $28.25

   c. Adel's Clothing   d. $15.50

B. Look at the ad and circle the correct answers.

1. How much is the blouse?

   a. $3.00

   b. $23.50

   c. $44.50

   d. $5.00

2. How much is the coat?

   a. $3.00

   b. $28.00

   c. $44.50

   d. $5.00

LESSON **1** **Where we live**

GOAL ■ Identify and ask about locations

A. Match the stores to the signs.

1.

2.

3.

4.

a.

b.

c.

d.

B. Write the words in alphabetical order (a–z).

shoe store	restaurant	bank	fast-food
bookstore	pharmacy	department store	convenience store
clothing store	hotel	supermarket	electronics store

1. _____ bank _____   2. _____

3. _____   4. _____

5. _____   6. _____

7. _____   8. _____

9. _____   10. _____

11. _____   12. _____

C. Circle the correct answer.

1. Where do you buy clothing?

   a. a bank   (b. a clothing store)   c. a pharmacy

2. Where do you buy medicine?

   a. a shoe store   b. a clothing store   c. a pharmacy

3. Where do you buy food?

   a. a shoestore   b. a clothing store   c. a supermarket

4. Where do you buy shoes?

   a. an electronics store   b. a pharmacy   c. a shoe store

5. Where do you buy a hamburger?

   a. a clothing store   b. a fast-food restaurant   c. a bookstore

D. Write answers in complete sentences for Exercise C.

1. I buy clothing at a clothing store. _____

2. _____

3. _____

4. _____

5. _____

E. Read the chart.

Yes/No Questions	
Questions	**Answers**
Do you buy clothing at a department store?	
Do you buy food at a supermarket?	
Do you buy shoes at a shoe store?	Yes, I do.
Do you live in Los Angeles?	No, I don't.
Do you need shoes?	
Do you need help?	

F. Check (✓) the correct answer.

1. Do you buy clothes at the supermarket?   ☐ Yes, I do.   ☐ No, I don't.

2. Do you buy electronics at the shoe store?   ☐ Yes, I do.   ☐ No, I don't.

3. Do you buy milk at the supermarket?   ☐ Yes, I do.   ☐ No, I don't.

4. Do you buy shoes at the supermarket?   ☐ Yes, I do.   ☐ No, I don't.

5. Do you buy medicine at the pharmacy?   ☐ Yes, I do.   ☐ No, I don't.

6. Do you buy cookies at the electronics store?   ☐ Yes, I do.   ☐ No, I don't.

G. Write the question.

1. _Do you_____ like milk and cookies? Yes, I like milk and cookies.

2. _____ live in San Francisco? No, I don't live in San Francisco.

3. _____ need help? Yes, I need help.

4. _____ live in Costa Mesa? No, I don't live in Costa Mesa.

5. _____ buy food at Jasper's Market? Yes, I buy food at Jasper's Market.

6. _____ like school? Yes, I like school.

H. Answer the questions about you.

1. Do you buy clothes at a department store? _____

2. Do you like milk? _____

3. Do you need new shoes? _____

4. Do you buy food for your family? _____

I. Write four of your own questions.

1. Do you _____?

2. Do you _____?

3. Do you _____?

4. Do you _____?

LESSON **2** Where do you live?

GOAL ■ Describe housing

A. Read the ads.

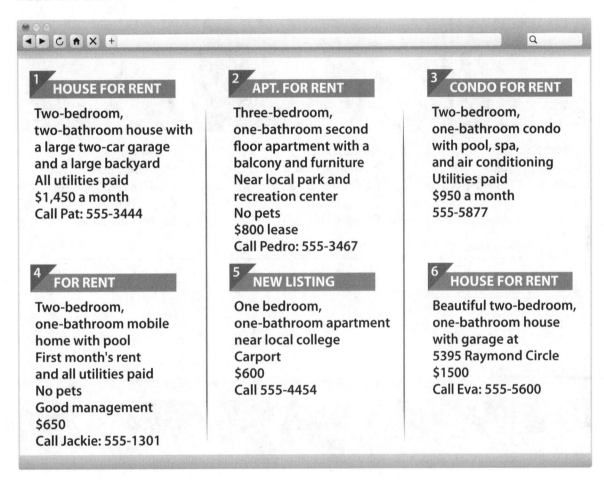

1 HOUSE FOR RENT

Two-bedroom,
two-bathroom house with
a large two-car garage
and a large backyard
All utilities paid
$1,450 a month
Call Pat: 555-3444

2 APT. FOR RENT

Three-bedroom,
one-bathroom second
floor apartment with a
balcony and furniture
Near local park and
recreation center
No pets
$800 lease
Call Pedro: 555-3467

3 CONDO FOR RENT

Two-bedroom,
one-bathroom condo
with pool, spa,
and air conditioning
Utilities paid
$950 a month
555-5877

4 FOR RENT

Two-bedroom,
one-bathroom mobile
home with pool
First month's rent
and all utilities paid
No pets
Good management
$650
Call Jackie: 555-1301

5 NEW LISTING

One bedroom,
one-bathroom apartment
near local college
Carport
$600
Call 555-4454

6 HOUSE FOR RENT

Beautiful two-bedroom,
one-bathroom house
with garage at
5395 Raymond Circle
$1500
Call Eva: 555-5600

B. Complete the table about Exercise A.

Contact	Housing type	How much?
1. Pat	house	$1,450
2.		
3.		
4.		
5.		
6.		

C. Look at the information and write sentences.

Name: Saud
Housing: house
Address: 2323 Hartford Rd.
City: Corbin
State: California

Name: Silvia
Housing: mobile home
Address: 13 Palm Ave.
City: Corbin
State: California

Name: Tien
Housing: apartment
Address: 15092 Arbor Lane #22
City: Corbin
State: California

1. Saud *lives in a house* _____.

2. Silvia _____.

3. Tien _____.

D. Read the chart.

In / On			
	Preposition		**Example sentence**
I live You live He lives She lives We live They live	in	a house an apartment a condo a mobile home	I live in a house. They live in an apartment. We live in a condo. She lives in a mobile home.
		a city	You live in Chicago.
		a state	They live in California.
	on	a street	I live on First Street. We live on Broadway. He lives on Main Street.

E. Write the words in the table.

| California | Birch Street | mobile home | house |
| Los Angeles | Walker Drive | West Palm St. | Second Street |

In	On

F. Check (✓) the correct answer.

1. Lien lives _____ an apartment. ☐ in ☐ on

2. They live _____ Texas. ☐ in ☐ on

3. We live _____ Main Street. ☐ in ☐ on

4. We have a house _____ Bush Avenue. ☐ in ☐ on

5. I live _____ a house. ☐ in ☐ on

6. He lives _____ Mexico City. ☐ in ☐ on

G. Write about Youssef.

I'm Youssef.
I'm from Saudi Arabia.
I live _____ a house.
I live _____ Market Street _____ San Francisco.

H. Write about you.

I'm _____.

I'm from _____.

I live _____.

I live _____.

LESSON **3** I take the bus

GOAL ■ Identify different types of transportation

A. Match the transportation with the verb.

1.

ride

2.

drive

3.

4.

take

B. Check (✓) the answers for you.

1. Do you drive to school?   ☐ Yes, I do.   ☐ No, I don't.

2. Do you take the bus to school?   ☐ Yes, I do.   ☐ No, I don't.

3. Do you walk to school?   ☐ Yes, I do.   ☐ No, I don't.

C. Read the conversations and complete the table.

Saud: How do you get to school?

Margaret: I take the train every day.

Saud: Every day?

Margaret: Yes. I do my homework on the train.

Margaret: How do you get to the doctor?

Nina: I drive.

Margaret: Oh, you have a car?

Nina: Yes, I do.

Nina: How do you get to the pharmacy?

Saud: I take the bus. I don't have a car.

Nina: I can drive you when you need to go.

Saud: Great! That helps a lot.

Name	Transportation	Destination
Saud		
Margaret		
Nina		

D. Read the chart.

Come to / Go to				
Subject	**Verb**	***to***	**Location**	**Example sentence**
I You We They	come go	to	work school the park	I **come** to work. We **go** to school. They **go** to the park.
			home	We **go** home. They **come** home.
He She	comes goes	to	work school the park	He **comes** to work. She **goes** to school. He **goes** to the park.
			home	He **goes** home. She **comes** home.

E. Write *comes* or *goes*.

1.

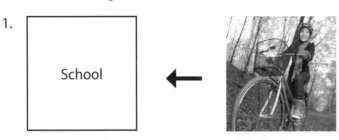

An ___*comes*___ to school at 10:00 a.m.

2.

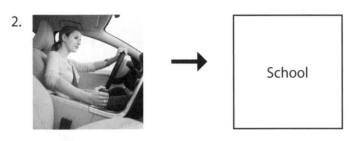

Carina _____ to school.

3.

James _____ to work.

F. Complete the sentences.

1. He _____ (come) to school.

2. She _____ (go) to work.

3. They _____ (go) to the store.

4. We _____ (come) home.

5. I _____ (come) to class at 10:00 a.m.

6. John and Marie _____ (go) together.

7. You _____ (go) at 3:00 p.m.

8. Marie _____ (come) late.

G. Answer the questions.

1. How do you get to school? I _____ to school.

2. When do you come to school? I _____ to school at _____.

3. What time do you go home? I _____ home at _____.

GOAL ■ Express personal information

A. Read the information and write paragraphs.

I'm James. I'm from the United States. I live in a house. I take the bus to school.

Name: James
From: United States
Housing: house
Transportation: bus

I'm An _____

_____

_____

_____

Name: An
From: Vietnam
Housing: house
Transportation: bicycle

I'm _Carina_ _____

_____

_____

_____

Name: Carina
From: Cuba
Housing: apartment
Transportation: car

B. Read.

Simple Present: The Verb *Be*		
Pronoun	***Be***	
I	am	I am An.
He, She, It,	is	She is from Vietnam.
We, You, They	are	They are married.

C. Write the correct form of the verb *Be*.

1. Ana _____is_____ from Mexico.

2. He _____ single.

3. They _____ married.

4. We _____ students.

5. They _____ from China.

6. I _____ a student.

D. Read the chart.

Simple Present		
Subject	**Verb**	**Example sentence**
I You We They	live (in/on) take ride walk (to)	I **live** in Mexico. We **take** the bus. They **take** a train. You **ride** a bicycle. I **walk** to school.
He She	lives (in/on) takes rides walks (to)	He **lives** on Main Street. She **takes** the bus. He **rides** a bicycle. She **walks** to the store.

E. Read the table and check (✓) the correct word.

Name	Transportation	Housing
Alfonso	train	house
Lien	bus	house
Casper	car	apartment
Carina	bicycle	condominium
Nadia	car	mobile home
Gilberto	bus	house
Gilda	walk	mobile home

1. Casper _____ to school. ☐ walks ☐ drives ☐ rides

2. Gilberto _____ a bus to school. ☐ rides ☐ takes ☐ drives

3. Alfonso _____ a train to school. ☐ walks ☐ drives ☐ takes

F. Look at Exercise E. Complete the sentences.

1. Alfonso _____lives_____ in a house, and he _____takes_____ the train to school.

2. Gilberto and Lien _____ in a house, and they _____ the bus to school.

3. Nadia and Gilda _____ in a mobile home.

4. Carina _____ a _____ to school.

5. _____ _____ in a condominium.

6. Nadia and Casper _____.

G. Complete the sentences.

1. Marvin _____rides_____ a bicycle to school.

2. You _____ a bus to the store.

3. Anya _____ a car to work.

4. I _____ to school.

5. Alexi and Humberto _____ the train to work.

6. Omar _____ in a house.

7. Peter and I _____ to the store.

8. Lien and Duong _____ on First Street.

GOAL ▪ Give and follow directions

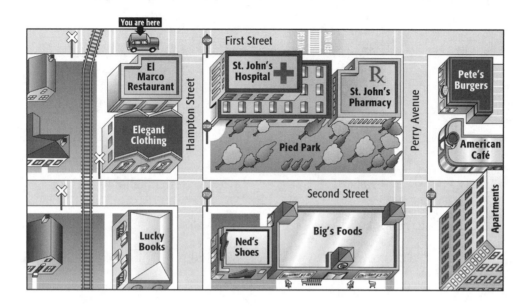

A. Look at the map and write the correct answer.

1. Ned's Shoes is next to _____.

2. St. John's Hospital is next to _____.

3. Elegant Clothing is on _____.

4. Pete's Burgers is on _____.

B. Read the directions. Circle the correct answer.

1. Go straight on First Street. Turn right on Hampton. It's next to the park.

   a. the restaurant

   b. the hospital

2. Go straight on First Street. Turn right on Hampton. Turn left on Second. It's next to Ned's Shoes.

   a. Big's Foods

   b. Lucky Boots

3. Go straight on First Street. Turn right on Perry Avenue. It's next to Pete's Burgers.

   a. the park

   b. American Café

C. Read the paragraph about Mary and write *a*, *b*, and *c* on the map.

Mary lives in Appleton. She walks to school every morning. Then she goes to work in the afternoon. She goes home at 6:00. She is very busy. (a) The school is on Hampton Street next to Food Mart. She works at the hospital. She is a nurse. (b) The hospital is on First Street next to the pharmacy. After work, she goes home. (c) Her apartment is on First Street next to the train tracks.

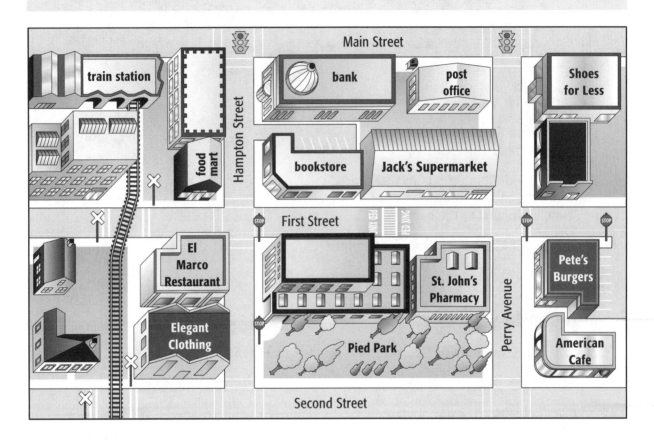

D. Read the chart.

Imperatives			
Subject	**Imperative**		**Example sentence**
~~you~~	stop		Stop.
	go	straight	Go straight.
	turn	left right around	Turn left. Turn right. Turn around.* *turn around = ↻

E. Look at the map and match the directions with the locations.

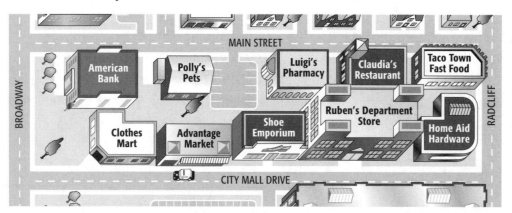

1. Start on City Mall Drive at the shoe store.

2. Go straight. Turn left on Radcliff. Go to the corner of Main Street.

3. Turn around. Go right on City Mall Drive. Turn right on Broadway. Turn right on Main Street. Stop next to the bank.

4. Go straight. Go to the restaurant between Luigi's Pharmacy and Taco Town Fast Food.

a. Polly's Pets

b. Shoe Emporium

c. Claudia's Restaurant

d. Taco Town Fast Food

F. Write sentences correctly.

1. go straight turn right on Second Street turn left on First Street stop

   Go straight. Turn right on Second Street. Turn left on First Street. Stop.

2. turn around go straight turn left turn right on Birch Avenue stop it's next to the market

   _____

   _____

G. Write directions to your house from your school.

   _____

   _____

   _____

   _____

   _____

PRACTICE TEST

A. Look at the map and circle the correct answers.

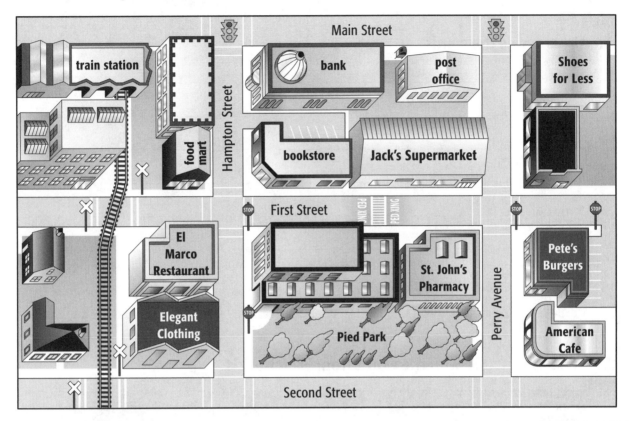

1. Where is the bookstore?
   a. next to the hospital
   b. on Main Street
   c. next to the bank
   d. next to the supermarket

2. Where's the post office?
   a. next to the train station
   b. on Main Street
   c. on First Street
   d. next to the restaurant

3. Where's the park?
   a. in front of the hospital
   b. on Main Street
   c. next to the bookstore
   d. next to Pete's burgers.

4. Where's the bank?
   a. on Perry Avenue
   b. next to the shoe store
   c. on Main Street
   d. on Second Street

LESSON 1 I need a checkup

GOAL ■ Identify body parts

A. Unscramble the words.

1. yese _____

2. deah _____

3. mra _____

4. tofo _____

5. mtouh _____

6. sneo _____

7. hnda _____

8. gle _____

B. Label the picture with the words from Exercise A.

C. **Match the pictures with the phrases. Draw a line.**

1.

a. Please *stand up.*

2.

b. Please *read* the chart.

3.

c. Please *sit down.*

4.

d. Please *open* your mouth.

D. **Read the chart.**

Imperatives			
	Subject	**Verb**	**Example sentence**
Please	~~you~~	read	Please read the chart.
		open	Please open your mouth.
		let me (look)	Please let me look in your ear.
		sit down	Please sit down.
		stand up	Please stand up.
Combinations: Please stand up and read the chart. Please sit down and let me look in your ear.			

E. Read and practice the conversation.

Doctor: Hello, Anya. Please sit down.

Anya: Thank you, doctor.

Doctor: How do you feel?

Anya: I feel fine.

Doctor: Please read the eye chart.

Anya: E . . . N . . . F . . . R . . . S

Doctor: Very good. Please open your mouth and say, "Ah."

Anya: Ah.

Doctor: Thank you.

F. Read what the doctor says. Draw a line to the correct response.

1. Please open your mouth and say, "Ah."   a. The right or left ear?

2. Please read the chart.   b. Ah.

3. Please let me look in your ear.   c. In this chair?

4. Please sit down.   d. Fine.

5. How do you feel?   e. E . . . N . . . F . . . R . . . S

G. Write a conversation.

Doctor: _____

Patient: _____

Doctor: _____

Patient: _____

Doctor: _____

Patient: _____

Doctor: _____

UNIT 6

L E S S O N **2** **I'm sick!**

GOAL ▪ Describe symptoms and illnesses

A. Read the paragraph and answer the questions.

> Chen is from China. He lives in the United States. He has a headache, a fever, and a sore throat. Sometimes his head hurts a lot and it makes his stomach ache, too. He needs a doctor, but he is nervous because he speaks only a little English.

1. Where is Chen from? _____

2. What is the matter? _____

3. Why is he nervous? _____

B. Look at the pictures and write Chen's symptoms.

_____ _____ _____

C. Write a conversation between Chen and the doctor.

Chen: _____

Doctor: _____

Chen: _____

Doctor: _____

Chen: _____

Doctor: _____

D. Read the table and complete the sentences.

Name	Headache	Stomachache	Backache	Fever	Cold
Humberto	X				X
Hue		X			
Chen	X		X		
Omar		X		X	

1. _____Humberto_____ has a headache and a cold.

2. _____ and _____ have headaches.

3. _____ has a stomachache and a fever.

4. _____ has a headache and a backache.

E. Read the charts.

Simple Present (Regular)		
Subject	Verb	Example sentence
I, You, We, They	**see** **visit**	I **see** the doctor once a year. We **visit** the doctor once a year.
He, She, It	**sees** **visits**	He **sees** the doctor once a week. She **visits** the doctor once a week.

Simple Present (Irregular)		
Subject	*Be*	Example sentence
I	**am**	I **am** sick.
You, We, They	**are**	We **are** sick.
He, She, It	**is**	He **is** sick.

Simple Present (Irregular)		
Subject	*Have*	Example sentence
I, You, We, They	**have**	I **have** a headache.
He, She, It	**has**	She **has** a runny nose.

F. Check (✓) the correct answer.

1. Guillermo _____ sick.   ☐ is   ☐ are   ☐ has   ☐ have

2. Maritza _____ a headache.   ☐ is   ☐ are   ☐ has   ☐ have

3. John _____ a runny nose.   ☐ is   ☐ are   ☐ has   ☐ have

4. We _____ sick.   ☐ is   ☐ are   ☐ has   ☐ have

5. Huong _____ healthy.   ☐ is   ☐ are   ☐ has   ☐ have

6. Mele _____ ill.   ☐ is   ☐ are   ☐ has   ☐ have

7. They _____ a fever.   ☐ is   ☐ are   ☐ has   ☐ have

8. Julio _____ a sore throat.   ☐ is   ☐ are   ☐ has   ☐ have

9. Maria and Claudia _____ colds.   ☐ is   ☐ are   ☐ has   ☐ have

10. We _____ very healthy.   ☐ is   ☐ are   ☐ has   ☐ have

G. Read the table.

	Guillermo	Antonio	Maritza
see a doctor	once a year	two times a year	three times a year
have a checkup	once a year	two times a year	once a year
visit the eye doctor	two times a year	two times a year	once a year
go to the hospital	once a year	three times a year	once a year

H. Complete the sentences.

1. Guillermo _____*sees*_____ the doctor _*once a year*_____.

2. Guillermo and Maritza _____ a checkup _____.

3. Antonio and Guillermo _____ the eye doctor _____.

4. Maritza _____ the eye doctor _____.

5. Guillermo and Maritza _____ to the hospital _____.

6. Antonio _____ the hospital _____.

7. Antonio _____ a checkup _____.

8. Maritza _____ the doctor _____.

LESSON **3** You need aspirin

GOAL ■ Identify medications

A. Read and answer the questions.

	Calender |∨	⊕ New |∨	Import	Share ∨	😀 ⚙

◀▶ **January 25th** | | View: Day ∨

	NAME	PROBLEM	PHONE
2:15 pm	**Hang Tran**	**Checkup**	**555-1235**
3:00 pm	**Elsa Kusmin**	**Headache**	**555-5842**
3:45 pm	**Orlando Ramirez**	**Leg hurts**	**555-3765**
4:30 pm	**Amal Jahsan**	**Backache**	**555-2220**
5:15 pm	**Fawzia Ahadi**	**Cold**	**555-9876**

1. Who has a checkup? _____

2. What is Fawzia's problem? _____

3. What time is Elsa's appointment? _____

4. What is Orlando's phone number? _____

5. What is the matter with Amal? _____

6. Who has a headache? _____

7. What is Elsa's phone number? _____

8. What time is Hang's appointment? _____

B. Look at the pictures and write the symptoms and medicines.

Symptom: _____headache_____ _____ _____

Medicine: _____aspirin_____ _____cold medicine_____ _____

C. Write medicines for the symptoms.

1. backache: _____aspirin_____

2. fever: _____

3. cough: _____

4. sore throat: _____

D. Read the chart.

Simple Present: *Need/Have*			
Subject	**Verb**		**Example sentence**
I, You, We, They	have	a headache	I have a headache.
	need	aspirin	They need aspirin.
He, She, It	has	a stomachache	He has a stomachache.
	needs	antacid	She needs antacid.
Combinations:	She has a headache. She needs aspirin. You have a stomachache. You need antacid. They have coughs. They need cough syrup.		

E.   Match the symptom and the medicine.

1. cough

2. headache

3. stomachache

F.   Complete the sentences.

1. He has a headache. He needs _____ .

2. She has a stomachache. She needs _____ .

3. Alicia has a cough. She needs _____ .

G.   Complete the sentences.

1. John _____has_____ a headache. He ____needs____ aspirin.

2. Melanie _____ a sore throat. She _____ cough syrup.

3. They _____ sore throats. They _____ _____ .

4. We _____ stomachaches. We _____ _____ .

5. I _____ a backache. I _____ _____ .

6. You _____ a runny nose. You _____ _____ .

7. Juan and Lien _____ headaches. They _____ _____ .

8. Alexi _____ a fever. He _____ _____ .

9. John and I _____ fevers. We _____ _____ .

10. She _____ a runny nose. She _____ _____ .

LESSON **4** Exercise every day!

GOAL ■ Describe healthy habits

A. Read about Julia and Delmar.

My name is Julia. I am forty years old and single. I sleep eight hours a night. I eat breakfast, lunch, and dinner. I exercise thirty minutes every day. I don't smoke. I get a checkup once a year. I think I am in good health.

This is Delmar. He is twenty-seven years old and married. He smokes. He doesn't get a checkup every year. He sleeps five hours a night. He eats breakfast, lunch, and dinner. He exercises twenty minutes every day. Dalmar is unhealthy.

B. Write the information in the diagram.

sleeps eight hours a night

exercises

sleeps five hours a night

smokes

gets a checkup once a year

eats breakfast, lunch, and dinner

is in good health

is unhealthy

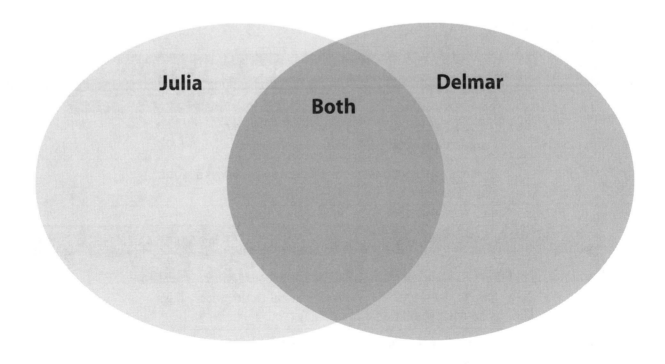

C. Read and complete the sentences.

Name: Huong
Sleep: 8 hours
Meals: breakfast, lunch, dinner
Exercise: 0 minutes a day
Checkup: 1 time a year
Smoke: yes

Name: Adriano
Sleep: 5 hours
Meals: breakfast, dinner
Exercise: 60 minutes a day
Checkup: 2 times a year
Smoke: no

Name: Aki
Sleep: 8 hours
Meals: breakfast, lunch, dinner
Exercise: 30 minutes a day
Checkup: 1 time a year
Smoke: no

1. Aki sleeps _____ hours every night.

2. Aki exercises _____ minutes every day.

3. Huong eats _____ times a day.

4. Adriano visits the doctor _____.

D. Read the charts.

Simple Present

Subject	Verb	Example sentence
I, You, We, They	sleep, eat, exercise, smoke, go	I eat three meals a day.
He, She, It	sleeps, eats, exercises, smokes, goes	She sleeps seven hours a night.

Negative Simple Present

Subject	Verb	Example sentence
I, You, We, They	don't sleep, eat, exercise, smoke, go	We don't eat three meals a day.
He, She, It	doesn't sleep, eat, exercise, smoke, go	He doesn't sleep seven hours a day.

E. Check (✓) the correct answers.

1. Ayumi and Julio _____ smoke. ☐ don't ☐ doesn't

2. He _____ have a checkup every year. ☐ don't ☐ doesn't

3. They _____ eat three meals a day. ☐ don't ☐ doesn't

4. Ayumi _____ eat fruit. ☐ don't ☐ doesn't

5. I _____ exercise every day. ☐ don't ☐ doesn't

6. We _____ sleep eight hours a night. ☐ don't ☐ doesn't

7. She _____ exercise 30 minutes a day. ☐ don't ☐ doesn't

8. Julio _____ smoke. ☐ don't ☐ doesn't

F. Change the verbs to the negative form.

1. Hasna eats two meals a day.

   She _doesn't eat_ _____ four meals a day.

2. Julia and Hasna have a checkup once a year.

   They _____ a checkup every month.

3. Julia and Dalmar sleep eight hours a day.

   They _____ ten hours.

4. Ayumi exercises three times a week.

   She _____ every day.

G. Complete the sentences about Exercise C.

1. Adriano _____ 60 minutes a day.

2. Huong _____ the doctor two times a year.

3. Huong and Aki _____ eight hours.

4. Aki and Adriano _____ smoke.

5. Huong and Aki _____ breakfast, lunch, and dinner.

LESSON **5** I have an appointment

GOAL ■ Identify actions in a waiting room

A. **Look at the picture and match the names with the verbs.**

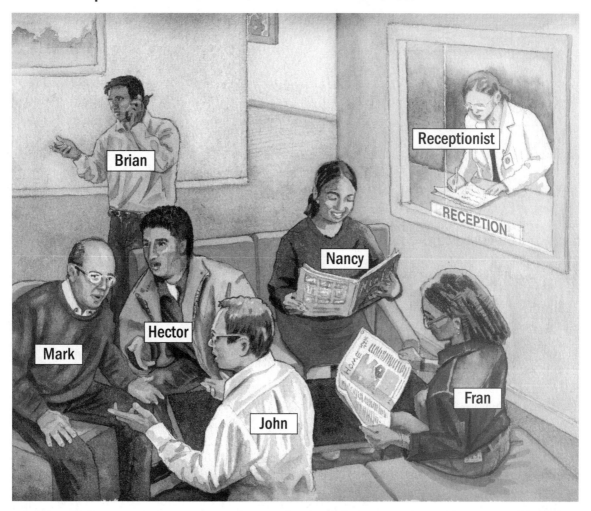

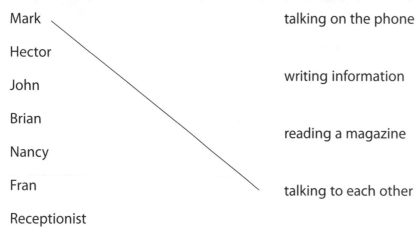

Mark   talking on the phone

Hector

John   writing information

Brian

Nancy   reading a magazine

Fran

Receptionist   talking to each other

B. **Look at the picture and write what the people are doing.**

1. _____ is reading a magazine.

2. _____ and _____ are talking.

3. _____ is sleeping.

4. The _____ is talking on the phone.

C. **Read the chart.**

Present Continuous			
Subject	*Be*	Base + *ing*	Example sentence
I	am	talking	I **am talking.**
He, She, It	is	sleeping	He **is sleeping.**
We, You, They	are	waiting	They **are waiting.**

D. Write the correct form of *Be*.

1. Huong _____ having lunch.

2. Richard _____ sleeping.

3. Ayumi and Fred _____ waiting.

4. They _____ talking.

5. I _____ answering the phone.

6. Julio _____ reading a book.

7. Delmar and Julia _____ talking.

8. You _____ waiting.

9. He _____ writing.

10. My friend and I _____ listening.

E. Complete the sentences about the picture in Exercise A. Use the words from the word box in the correct form. They can be used more than once.

read	talk	wait	sit	stand

1. The receptionist _____ is writing _____ information.

2. Nancy and Fran _____ magazines.

3. Mark, Hector, and John _____ to each other.

4. Brian _____ on the phone.

5. Everyone _____ for the doctor.

6. Mark, Hector, John, Nancy, and Fran _____.

7. The receptionist _____ in the window.

PRACTICE TEST

A. Read and circle the correct answers.

> Dr. Ames sees a lot of patients every day. Tuba has a sore throat and a headache. Oscar has a very high fever. Cynthia has a cold and runny nose. Abigail has a stomachache. They are all sick, and now the doctor is, too.

1. How many people are sick?
   - a. 5
   - b. 4
   - c. 3
   - d. 2

2. Who has a cold?
   - a. Oscar
   - b. Cynthia
   - c. runny nose
   - d. sick

B. Look at the medicine bottles and circle the correct answers.

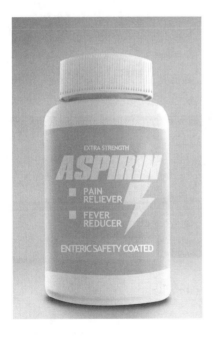 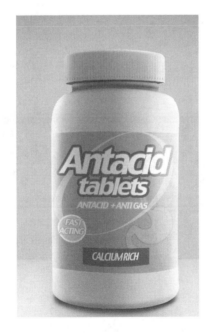 

1. Which is the medicine for a stomachache?
   - a. antacid
   - b. pain reliever
   - c. cough syrup
   - d. aspirin

2. Which is the medicine for a headache?
   - a. antacid
   - b. extra strength
   - c. calcium rich
   - d. aspirin

LESSON **1** Do you work?

GOAL ▇ Identify occupations

A. Look at the information and write sentences.

Name: Luisa
Occupation: cashier
Workplace: supermarket

Name: Pete
Occupation: teacher
Workplace: school

Name: Isabel
Occupation: receptionist
Workplace: office

Name: Vache
Occupation: salesperson
Workplace: clothing store

Name: Ivan
Occupation: custodian
Workplace: office building

Name: Ben
Occupation: nurse
Workplace: hospital

1. Luisa _is a cashier_____. She works _in a supermarket_____.

2. Pete _____. He works _____.

3. Isabel _____. She works _____.

4. Vache _____. He works _____.

5. Ivan _____. He works _____.

6. Ben _____. He works _____.

B. Complete the table with words from the box.

cashier	principal	secretary	receptionist	teacher	doctor
nurse	salesperson	manager	custodian	server	student

Supermarket	Office	Hospital	Restaurant	School

C. Add more jobs to the table in Exercise B.

D. Read the charts.

Simple Present		
Subject	Verb	Example sentence
I, You, We, They	work	I work. I am a teacher.
He, She, It	works	He works. He is a cashier.

Negative Simple Present		
Subject	Verb	Example sentence
I, You, We, They	don't work	We don't work.
He, She, It	doesn't work	He doesn't work.

E. Check (✓) the correct answer.

1. Vache _____ in a store on First Street. ☐ work ☐ works

2. Louisa and Vache _____ at Sam's Clothing. ☐ work ☐ works

3. I _____ in a factory. ☐ work ☐ works

4. We _____ at a school in Yorba City. ☐ work ☐ works

5. You _____ with children. ☐ work ☐ works

6. Ben _____ in the morning. ☐ work ☐ works

7. They _____ in a supermarket. ☐ work ☐ works

8. Chen _____ for a school. ☐ work ☐ works

F. Look at the pictures and complete the conversations.

Name: Esteban
Occupation: Delivery Person
Workplace: Fast-Xpress Delivery

Name: Ivan
Occupation: Custodian
Workplace: Freemont School

Name: Amy
Occupation: Gardener
Workplace: Freemont School

1. **A:** Where does Esteban work?

   B: He _works at Fast-Xpress Delivery_____.

2. **A:** Where does Amy work?

   B: She _____.

3. **A:** Where does Ivan work?

   B: He _____.

4. **A:** Where do Amy and Ivan work?

   B: They _____.

LESSON **2** When do you go to work?

GOAL ■ Give information about work

A. Read the paragraphs and circle the correct answers.

My name is Ben. I'm a nurse. I work at a hospital from 7:00 a.m. to 7:00 p.m. I work Monday through Thursday. I help the doctors and patients. My supervisor is Dr. O'Malley.

My name is Hue. I'm a doctor. I work at a hospital from 7:00 a.m. to 7:00 p.m. I work Friday through Sunday. I help patients. I am the supervisor.

1. Where do Ben and Angelina work?

    a. in a hospital   b. in an office   c. at 7:00 a.m.

2. Who is the nurse?

    a. Ben   b. doctor   c. Hue

3. When does Hue work?

    a. Monday–Thursday   b. Friday–Sunday   c. Friday and Sunday only

4. What is Hue's job?

    a. nurse   b. patients   c. doctor and supervisor

B. **Look at the table and complete the diagram.**

Ben	Hue
works in a hospital	works in a hospital
nurse	doctor
works Monday–Thursday	works Friday–Sunday
works from 7 a.m.–7 p.m.	works from 7 a.m.–7 p.m.
helps patients	helps patients
helps the doctor	supervises

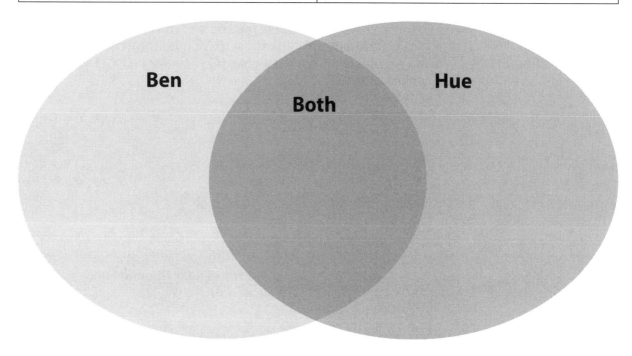

C. **Read the chart.**

Information Questions			
Question word	Type of answer	Example question	Answer
What	information (receptionist)	What do you do?	I am a receptionist.
Where	a place (Johnson Company)	Where do you work?	Johnson Company.
When	a time or day (9–6) (Monday–Friday)	When do you work?	On Monday at 5:00.
Who	a person (Martin Smith)	Who is your teacher?	Mr. Smith.

D. Check (✓) the correct answer.

1. Where does she work?

☐ Roxy's Department Store ☐ at 8:00 a.m. ☐ I am a custodian.

2. When do they go to work?

☐ Eric Johnson ☐ in an adult school ☐ at 6:30 p.m.

3. What does she do?

☐ She's a nurse. ☐ in a supermarket ☐ Oscar

4. Who is your supervisor?

☐ I'm a cashier. ☐ Mr. Peabody ☐ in the store

5. When does she go home?

☐ at 3:30 p.m. ☐ on 17th Street ☐ Maria

6. Who works at Addey's Clothing Store?

☐ I'm a salesperson. ☐ clothing store ☐ Lien

E. Match the questions to the answers.

1. Where do you work?

2. What do you do?

3. What does he do?

4. Where do they work?

5. Where does she work?

6. When does she finish work?

7. When does he start?

8. Who is your supervisor?

a. He's a custodian.

b. They work at a school.

c. She finishes at 5:00 p.m.

d. I'm a manager.

e. He starts at 11:00 p.m.

f. My supervisor is Natalia.

g. I work in a bank.

h. She works in a pharmacy.

LESSON **3** What do you do?

GOAL ■ Identify job duties

A. Match.

1. A salesperson   a. works in a school.
2. A student   b. talks to customers.
3. A teacher   c. works in a supermarket.
4. A cashier   d. works in a hospital.
5. A nurse   e. studies in a school.
6. A manager   f. works in an office.

B. Write sentences from Exercise A.

1. _A salesperson talks to customers._
2. _____
3. _____
4. _____
5. _____
6. _____

C. Look at the occupations. Write the occupations for the duties.

nurse	receptionist	~~doctor~~	custodian

	takes care of patients	helps the doctor	cleans	sends memos	schedules meetings
doctor	x				
	x	x			
				x	x
			x		

D. Write sentences from Exercise C.

1. *A doctor takes care of patients.* _____

2. _____

3. _____

4. _____

E. Complete the table.

	delivers packages	works outside	answers phones	counts money	talks to people
gardener					
delivery person					
receptionist					
cashier					

F. Write sentences from Exercise E.

1. _____

2. _____

3. _____

4. _____

G. Read the chart.

Modal: *Can / Can't*			
Subject	*Can*	Verb (base)	Example sentence
I, You, He, She, It, We, They	can	type	I can type.
		mop	He can mop floors.
Subject	*Can't*	Verb (base)	Example sentence
I, You, He, She, It, We, They	can't	type	I can't type.
		mop	He can't mop floors.

H. Read the table.

	Emilio	Carolina	Ahmed
type	no	yes	yes
drive	yes	yes	yes
count money	yes	no	yes
use a computer	yes	yes	no

I. Complete the sentences with *can* or *can't*.

1. Carolina _____*can*_____ type.

2. Emilio _____ drive.

3. Emilio and Carolina _____ drive.

4. Ahmed _____ use a computer.

5. Carolina _____ use a computer.

6. Emilio _____ count money and use the computer.

7. Emilio, Carolina, and Ahmed _____ drive.

8. Emilio _____ type.

J. Complete the sentences. Use *can* or *can't* and a verb from the box.

drive	help	come	schedule	speak

1. Emilio is sick. He _____ to work today.

2. Carolina is a good student. She _____ English well.

3. Chen is a good driver. He _____ a bus.

4. Hue is a good doctor. Lisa is a good nurse. They _____ patients.

5. Amy is a good receptionist. She _____ meetings.

K. Write what you can and can't do.

1. I can _____.

2. I can't _____.

LESSON **4** You're doing great!

GOAL ■ Read evaluations

A. Read Amy's evaluation and look at the evaluation form.

Amy is a good worker. She always helps customers and comes to work on time. Amy speaks to customers very clearly. Her English is very good. I never have to worry about Amy. She always follows directions.

NATIONAL SALES CORPORATION
Employee Evaluation Form

Name: **Amy Ochoa**

Position: **Receptionist**

Date: **June 27th**

Helps customers	(Yes)	No
Comes to work on time	(Yes)	No
Speaks English well	(Yes)	No
Follows directions well	(Yes)	No

Supervisor: *Kenny Gomez*

B. Answer the questions about Amy's evaluation.

1. What is the name of Amy's supervisor? _____

2. Does Amy follow directions? _____

3. What is the date? _____

4. Does Amy come to work on time? _____

5. Where does Amy work? _____

6. Does Amy speak English well? _____

C. Read the work evaluation.

WORK EVALUATION

Name: Peter Langdon

Helpful	(Yes)	No
Prompt (comes to work on time)	Yes	(No)
Friendly	(Yes)	No
Careful	Yes	(No)

Manager: *Calvin Carter*

D. Answer the questions about the evaluation.

1. Who is the worker? _____

2. Who is the manager? _____

3. Is Peter friendly? _____

4. Is Peter prompt? _____

E. Read the charts.

Be (affirmative)		
Subject	**Be**	**Example sentence**
I	am	I **am** friendly.
He, She, It	is	She **is** friendly.
We, You, They	are	They **are** friendly.

Be (negative)		
Subject	**Be (negative)**	**Example sentence**
I	am not	I **am not** friendly.
He, She, It	is not	She **is not** friendly.
We, You, They	are not	They **are not** friendly.

F. Check (✓) the correct verb.

1. John _____ friendly and prompt.   ☐ am   ☐ is   ☐ are

2. The salesperson _____ helpful.   ☐ am   ☐ is   ☐ are

3. I _____ careful.   ☐ am   ☐ is   ☐ are

4. We _____ friendly.   ☐ am   ☐ is   ☐ are

5. Margo and Stan _____ helpful.   ☐ am   ☐ is   ☐ are

6. You _____ very friendly.   ☐ am   ☐ is   ☐ are

G. Read the table and complete the sentences.

	Emilio	Carolina	Ahmed
friendly	no	yes	yes
helpful	yes	no	yes
prompt	yes	no	no
careful	yes	yes	no

1. Emilio _____ is not _____ friendly.

2. Ahmed and Carolina _____ prompt.

3. Carolina _____ careful.

4. Ahmed and Emilio _____ helpful.

5. Ahmed _____ careful.

6. Carolina _____ helpful or prompt.

H. Complete the evaluation about you.

EVALUATION		
Helpful	Yes	No
Prompt (comes to work on time)	Yes	No
Friendly	Yes	No
Careful	Yes	No

L E S S O N **5** Please send the memo

GOAL ■ Follow directions

A. Read the list of phrases for English class. Write each phrase in the correct column.

~~ask for help~~	speak only English	eat in the classroom
~~leave early~~	do homework	speak in your language
practice every day	come late to class	help others

Do's	Don'ts
ask for help	leave early

B. Complete the paragraph about do's and don'ts in the classroom.

It is important to follow the rules in English class. Pete is the teacher, and he asks the students to follow the rules so they can learn English well. He says to _____ only English in the class. Also, _____ your homework. He says to _____ on time and _____ _____ early. The school rules say _____ _____ in the classroom—eat outside.

C. Read the job description.

> ### Sam's Emporium
> **Job Title:** <u>Salesperson</u>
>
> 1. Come to work on time.
> 2. Help customers.
> 3. Speak English.
> 4. Don't eat in the store.
> 5. Don't leave early.
> 6. Don't smoke in the store.

D. Complete the table using the job description in Exercise C.

Do's	Don'ts

E. Read the chart.

Imperative			
Subject	**Verb**		**Example sentence**
You	wash	your hands	Wash your hands.
	answer	the phones	Answer the phones.
	type	the letters	Type the letters.
Negative Imperative			
Subject	**Verb**		**Example sentence**
You	don't	file	papers	Don't file papers.
		answer	the phones	Don't answer the phones.
		type	the letters	Don't type the letters.

F. Match the jobs with the commands.

_d, i_ 1. custodian

_____ 2. receptionist

_____ 3. cashier

_____ 4. doctor

_____ 5. salesperson

_____ 6. bus driver

a. Answer the phones.
b. Count the money.
c. Talk to patients.
d. Clean the floors.
e. Drive carefully.
f. Help the customers.
g. Look at street signs.
h. Give change.
i. Fix the chairs.
j. Schedule meetings.
k. Write the symptoms.
l. Check the inventory.

G. Complete the commands for the receptionist and the student. Use the verbs from the boxes. Make them negative when needed.

Receptionist:

eat	take	answer	talk	come

1. _____ lunch at your desk.

2. _____ the phones.

3. _____ to customers.

4. _____ to work late

5. _____ a two-hour lunch break.

Student:

forget	ask	do	speak	come

1. _____ to class late.

2. _____ your homework.

3. _____ English in class.

4. _____ your books.

5. _____ questions.

A. Read the evaluation and circle the correct answers.

Name: Davit Deluse		
Work Evaluation		
Question	Yes	No
1. Helps customers	✓	
2. Comes to work on time		✓
3. Is friendly	✓	
4. Is careful		✓
Manager Signature: Calvin Carter		

1. What does Davit do well?

   a. He is careful and late to work.

   b. He is not careful.

   c. He helps customers and is friendly.

   d. He comes to work on time.

2. What does Davit not do well?

   a. He helps customers.

   b. He does not come to work on time.

   c. He is not friendly.

   d. He is careful.

B. Look at the job description and circle the correct answers.

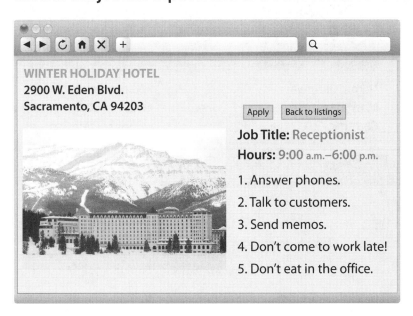

WINTER HOLIDAY HOTEL
2900 W. Eden Blvd.
Sacramento, CA 94203

[Apply] [Back to listings]

Job Title: Receptionist
Hours: 9:00 a.m.–6:00 p.m.

1. Answer phones.
2. Talk to customers.
3. Send memos.
4. Don't come to work late!
5. Don't eat in the office.

1. What is the job title?

   a. Receptionist   b. #33   c. Sacramento   d. 9:00 a.m.–6:00 p.m.

2. What is the name of the company?

   a. Sacramento   b. Receptionist   c. 9:00 a.m.–6:00 p.m.   d. Winter Holiday Hotel

LESSON **1** Let's get organized!

GOAL ■ Organize study materials

A. Look at the personal information and complete the table.

Name: Julia
Marital status: single
Native country: Mexico

Name: Hasna
Marital status: married
Native country: Saudi Arabia

Name: Dalmar
Marital status: single
Native country: Haiti

Name: Eva
Marital status: divorced
Country: Croatia

Name: Gabriela
Marital status: single
Country: Colombia

Name: Felipe
Marital status: married
Country: Mexico

Name	Marital status	Native country
Julia		

B. Complete the online profile page with your information.

Date of Birth: _____

Birthplace: _____

Address: _____

_____

City: _____

First Name: _____   State: _____

Last Name: _____   Zip: _____

C. Read the charts.

The Verb *Be*			
Subject	***Be***	**Information**	**Example sentence**
I	am	married	I am married. *(I'm married.)*
My phone number The address	is	555-3765	My phone number is 555-3765.
		2900 W. Adams	The address is 2900 W. Adams.
We You They	are	from Canada	We are from Canada. *(We're from Canada.)*
		married	You are married. *(You're married.)*
		divorced	They are divorced. *(They're divorced.)*

Questions with *What*			
Question word	***Be***	**Information**	**Example question**
What	is	your phone number	What's your phone number?
		your address	What's your address?

D. Check (✓) the correct answer.

1. I _____ Francisco Lozano.   ☐ am   ☐ is   ☐ are

2. My name _____ Francisco Lozano.   ☐ am   ☐ is   ☐ are

3. They _____ married.   ☐ am   ☐ is   ☐ are

4. We _____ from Venezuela.   ☐ am   ☐ is   ☐ are

5. The teacher's phone number _____ 555-3721.   ☐ am   ☐ is   ☐ are

6. Our address _____ 2900 W. Main Street.   ☐ am   ☐ is   ☐ are

7. You _____ a good student.   ☐ am   ☐ is   ☐ are

8. His name _____ Lars.   ☐ am   ☐ is   ☐ are

9. I _____ divorced.   ☐ am   ☐ is   ☐ are

10. Justin and I _____ friendly to customers.   ☐ am   ☐ is   ☐ are

E. Look at the information in Exercise A and write sentences.

1. Julia is single. _____.
2. Gabriela and Julia . . . _____.
3. _____
4. _____
5. _____
6. _____
7. _____
8. _____
9. _____
10. _____
11. _____
12. _____

F. Write sentences about your information in Exercise B.

1. I am _____.
2. My address is _____.
3. _____
4. _____
5. _____
6. _____

LESSON **2** I need paper

GOAL ■ Make purchases

A. Read the advertisement and complete the table.

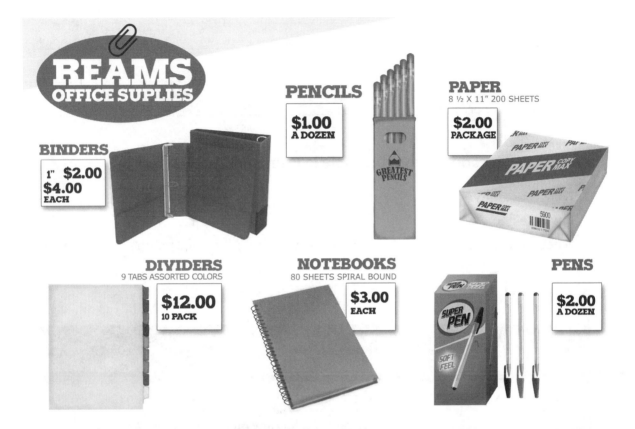

Reams Office Supplies			
Quantity	Packaging	Item	Unit price
540			$1.00
201	a dozen		$2.00
75		9-tab dividers	
33		binders	
310			$2.00
140	each		$3.00

B. **Complete the sentences about Exercise A.**

1. Pencils are _$1.00 a dozen_____.

2. Black ballpoints are _____.

3. 9-tab dividers are _____.

4. 1" binders are _____.

5. Paper is _____.

6. 80-sheet notebooks are _____.

C. **Answer the questions about the table in Exercise A.**

1. What is quantity?   ☐ how many   ☐ the price for one   ☐ a description
2. What are items?   ☐ how many   ☐ the price for one   ☐ a description
3. What is unit price?   ☐ how many   ☐ the price for one   ☐ a description

D. **Read the charts.**

How much			
Question word	**Be**	**Information**	**Example question**
How much (money)	**is**	the notebook	How much is the notebook?
		the paper	How much is the paper?
	are	the notebooks	How much are the notebooks?
		the dividers	How much are the dividers?
		the pencils	How much are the pencils?

How many			
Question word	**Information**		**Example question**
How many	notebooks	are there	How many notebooks are there?
	packages of paper		How many packages of paper are there?
	pencils		How many pencils are there?
	dividers		How many packs of dividers are there?

E. Match the questions with the answers. Look at Exercise A.

1. How much are the pencils?   a. 310
2. How many notebooks are there?   b. 201
3. How many packages of paper are there? c. $1.00 a dozen
4. How much are the pens?   d. 75
5. How much are the dividers?   e. $2.00 a dozen
6. How many dozens of pencils are there? f. $3.00 each
7. How much is the paper?   g. 540
8. How many dozens of pens are there?   h. $12.00 a pack
9. How many packs of dividers are there? i. $2.00 a package
10. How much are the notebooks?   j. 140

F. Check (✓) the correct answer.

1. How much _____ the notebooks?   ☐ is   ☐ are

2. How much _____ the pencils?   ☐ is   ☐ are

3. How much _____ a notebook?   ☐ is   ☐ are

4. How much _____ the binder?   ☐ is   ☐ are

5. How much _____ the pens?   ☐ is   ☐ are

6. How much _____ the paper?   ☐ is   ☐ are

7. How much _____ the binders?   ☐ is   ☐ are

8. How much _____ the dividers?   ☐ is   ☐ are

G. Make a shopping list using the ad in Exercise A. You have $20. What will you buy for school?

Quantity	Item	Total

LESSON **3** **Where's the office supply store?**

GOAL ■ Give and follow directions

A. Read the directory and answer the questions.

Palm City Government Agencies and Services

City Hall			**Library (Public)**	
160 W. Broadway	555-3300		125 E. Broadway	555-7323
Courthouse			**Playgrounds and Parks**	
150 W. Broadway	555-5245		**Department of Parks and Recreation**	
DMV (Department of Motor Vehicles)			160 W. Broadway, Suite 15	555-7275
Information	555-2227		**Angel Park**	
Appointments			137 Monroe St.	555-3224
375 Western Ave.	555-2778		**Lilly Community Park**	
U.S. Post Office			275 Carpenter	555-2211
151 E. Broadway	555-6245		**Schools (Public)**	
Fire Department			**Jefferson Middle**	
145 W. Broadway	555-3473		122 Jefferson St.	555-2665
Police Department			**Lincoln High**	
140 W. Broadway	555-4867		278 Lincoln Ave.	555-8336
Emergencies call 911			**Washington Elementary**	
			210 Washington St.	555-5437

1. What is the phone number for the fire department?

_____

2. What is the phone number for Angel Park?

_____

3. What is at 555-7323?

_____

4. What is the address for Jefferson Middle School?

_____

5. What is the address for the post office?

_____

6. What is located at 140 W. Broadway?

_____

B. **Read the map and answer the questions.**

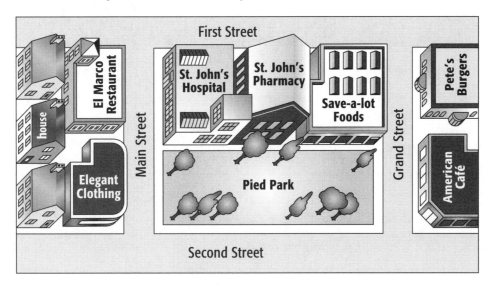

1. Which street is St. John's Pharmacy on? _____

2. Which street is Elegant Clothing on? _____

3. Which street is American Café on? _____

C. **Read the chart.**

Prepositions of Location		
	Preposition	**Example sentence**
St. John's Hospital / St. John's Pharmacy	next to	St. John's Hospital is **next to** St. John's Pharmacy.
St. John's Hospital / St. John's Pharmacy / Save-a-lot Foods	between	St. John's Pharmacy is **between** St. John's Hospital and Save-a-lot Foods.
El Marco Restaurant	on the corner	El Marco Restaurant is **on the corner** of Main Street and First Street.

D. Complete the table. Use the map in Exercise B.

Location	is next to ...	is between ...	is on the corner of ...
El Marco Restaurant	Elegant Clothing		Main Street and First Street
St. John's Pharmacy			
Pete's Burgers			
American Café			
St. John's Hospital			

E. Complete the sentences about the map in Exercise B.

1. American Café is _____ Grand Street.

2. Elegant Clothing is _____ of Main Street and Second Street.

3. Pete's Burgers is _____ American Café.

4. St. John's Pharmacy is _____ Save-a-lot Foods.

5. El Marco Restaurant is _____ Main.

6. American Café is _____ Grand Street and Second Street.

7. _____ is between St. John's Hospital and Save-a-lot Foods.

8. _____ is next to Elegant Clothing.

F. Write the locations of places in your community.

1. The school is _____.

2. The bank is _____.

3. The supermarket is _____.

4. The hospital is _____.

LESSON **4** Sleep eight hours a night

GOAL ■ Make goals

A. Read about Frank's and Cathy's goals. Complete the diagram.

Frank	Cathy
• sleep eight hours	• sleep seven hours
• go to school every day	• go to school every day
• exercise two hours a day	• exercise one hour a day
• study English at home every day	• study English at home every day
• read an English newspaper every day	• read the Internet in English every day
• watch TV in English	• watch TV in English

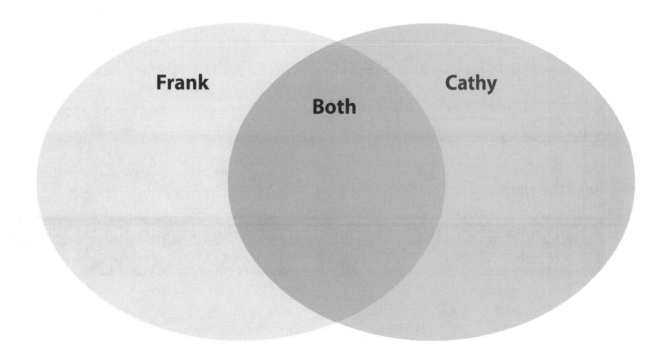

B. Read the graph and answer the questions.

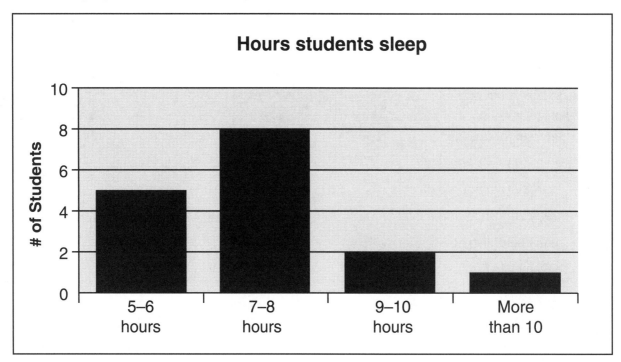

1. How many students sleep 9–10 hours a night? _____

2. How many students sleep 5–6 hours a night? _____

3. How many hours do you sleep a night? _____

C. Read the chart.

Simple Present			
Subject	**Verb**		**Example sentence**
I, You, We, They	exercise walk work study sleep	three times a week every day on Monday eight hours a day in the morning	I exercise three times a week. We walk on Monday. They work every day. You study in the morning. I sleep eight hours a night.
He, She, It	exercises walks works studies sleeps		He exercises on Monday. She walks every day. She works three times a week. He studies one hour in the morning. He sleeps eight hours a night.

D. **Complete the sentences with the correct form of the verb.**

1. John _____ (exercise) every day.

2. They _____ (sleep) six hours every night.

3. He _____ (study) in the morning.

4. I _____ (study) three times a week.

5. She _____ (work) in the afternoon.

6. We _____ (walk) to the park on Saturdays.

E. **Read about Melinda's and Duong's health habits and complete the sentences.**

Melinda	Duong
Exercise: 2 hours a day **Eat:** 3 meals a day **Sleep:** 8 hours a night **Study:** 1 hour a day	**Exercise:** 1 hour a day **Eat:** 2 meals a day **Sleep:** 8 hours a night **Study:** 1 hour a day

1. Melinda _____ two hours a day.

2. Melinda and Duong _____ one hour a day.

3. They _____ eight hours a night.

4. Duong _____ two meals a day.

5. Melinda _____ one hour a day.

6. Melinda _____ three meals a day.

F. **Write about your health habits.**

1. I exercise _____.

2. I eat _____.

3. I sleep _____.

4. I study _____.

LESSON ⑤ When can I study?

GOAL ▦ Develop a study schedule

A. Read the schedule and answer the questions.

ALI'S SCHEDULE

	Sunday	Monday	Tuesday	Wednesday	Thursday	Friday	Saturday
6:00 A.M.							
9:00 A.M.		School		School		School	
11:00 A.M.							
1:00 P.M.		Work	Work	Work	Work	Work	
3:00 P.M.							
5:00 P.M.	Dinner	Dinner	Dinner	Dinner	Dinner	Dinner	Dinner
7:00 P.M.	Study	Study	Study	Study	Study	Study	

1. When does Ali study at school?

   Ali studies at school on Monday, Wednesday, and Friday.

2. When does he work?

   _____.

3. When does he study at home?

   _____.

4. When does he have dinner?

   _____.

5. Does he go to school on Saturday?

   _____.

B. Read the schedule and complete the table.

Mario's Afternoon Schedule					
	Monday	Tuesday	Wednesday	Thursday	Friday
12:00 p.m.	Lunch	Lunch	Lunch	Lunch	Lunch
1:00 p.m.	Study	Study	Study	Study	Study
2:00 p.m.	School	School	School	School	
3:00 p.m.	School	School	School	School	
4:00 p.m.	Walk	Exercise	Exercise	Exercise	Walk

2 times a week	3 times a week	4 times a week	5 times a week
walk			

C. Read the chart.

Simple Present			
Subject	Verb		Example sentence
I, You, We, They	exercise walk work sleep study go have	three times a week every day on Monday at 8 a.m. in the morning in the afternoon at night	I exercise three times a week. We walk on Monday. They work at 8 a.m. I sleep eight hours every night. You study at night. They go to school in the morning. We have lunch in the afternoon.
He, She, It	exercises walks works sleeps studies goes has		He exercises on Monday. She walks every day. She works at 8 a.m. He sleeps eight hours every night. He studies at night. She goes to school in the morning. He has lunch in the afternoon.

D. **Complete the sentences with the correct form of the verb.**

1. Omar _____ (eat) lunch with a friend every Monday.

2. Kenny _____ (exercise) four times a week.

3. They _____ (work) at night.

4. We _____ (study) every night.

5. You _____ (have) school at 2:00 p.m.

6. I _____ (exercise) every morning at 5:00 a.m.

E. **Complete the paragraph about Chen's morning schedule. Use verbs from the box.**

Chen's Morning Schedule					
	Monday	Tuesday	Wednesday	Thursday	Friday
6:00 a.m.	Breakfast	Breakfast	Breakfast	Breakfast	Breakfast
9:00 a.m.	School	School	School	School	Study
11:00 a.m.	Lunch	Lunch	Lunch	Lunch	Lunch
12:00 p.m.	Study	Study	Study	Study	Study

work	eat	study	have	go

Chen is a good student. He _____ breakfast at 6:00 a.m. every day. He

_____ to school four times a week. He _____ lunch between 11:00 a.m.

and 12:00 p.m. every day. He _____ at 12:00 p.m. every day. Chen works very hard.

F. **Write your morning schedule.**

My Morning Schedule					
	Monday	Tuesday	Wednesday	Thursday	Friday
6:00 a.m.					
9:00 a.m.					
11:00 a.m.					
12:00 p.m.					

A. Read the schedule and circle the correct answers.

LIANG'S SCHEDULE

	Sunday	Monday	Tuesday	Wednesday	Thursday	Friday	Saturday
6:00 a.m.	Breakfast	Breakfast	Breakfast	Breakfast	Breakfast	Breakfast	Breakfast
9:00 a.m.		School	School	School	School	Study	Study
11:00 a.m.	Lunch	Lunch	Lunch	Lunch	Lunch	Lunch	Lunch
1:00 p.m.		Study	Study	Study	Study	Study	Study
3:00 p.m.							
5:00 p.m.		Work	Work	Work	Work	Work	
7:00 p.m.	Dinner	Dinner	Dinner	Dinner	Dinner	Dinner	Dinner
9:00 p.m.							

1. When does Liang eat every day?

   a. at 6:00 a.m., 11:00 a.m., and 7:00 p.m.   b. at 6:00 p.m., 11:00 p.m., and 7:00 p.m.

   c. at 1:00 p.m.   d. at 12:00 p.m.

2. When does Liang go to school?

   a. at night   b. in the morning

   c. in the afternoon   d. at 9:00 p.m.

B. Read the ad and circle the correct answers.

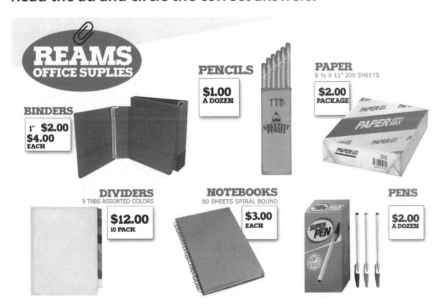

1. How much is the paper?

   a. 8½ x 11   b. $2.00   c. 200 sheets   d. college rule

2. How many pens are in a box?

   a. ballpoint   b. $2.00   c. 12   d. a box

GLOSSARY OF GRAMMAR TERMS

adjective	a word that describes a noun (Example: the _red_ hat)
adverb	a word that modifies a verb, adjective, or another adverb (Example: She eats _quickly_.)
affirmative	not negative and not a question (Example: _I like him._)
apostrophe	a punctuation mark that shows missing letters in contractions or possession (Example: _It's_ or _Jim's_)
article	words used before a noun (Example: _a, an, the_)
base form	the main form of a verb, used without _to_ (Example: _be, have, study_)
comma	a punctuation mark used to indicate a pause or separation (Example: I live in an apartment, and you live in a house.)
complement	a word or words that add to or complete an idea after the verb (Example: He is _happy_.)
conjugation	the form of a verb (Example: I _am_, You _are_, We _are_, They _are_, He _is_, She _is_, It _is_)
continuous form	a verb form that expresses action during time (Example: He _is shopping_.)
contraction	shortening of a word, syllable, or word group by omission of a sound or letter (Example: It is = _It's_, does not = _doesn't_)
count nouns	nouns that can be counted by number (Example: one _apple_, two _apples_)
definite article	use of _the_ when a noun is known to speaker and listener (Example: I know _the_ store.)
exclamation mark	a punctuation symbol marking surprise or emotion (Example: Hello_!_)
formal	polite or respectful language (Example: _Could_ you _please_ give me that?)
imperative	a command form of a verb (Example: _Listen_! or _Look out_!)
indefinite article	_a_ or _an_ used before a noun when something is talked about for the first time or when _the_ is too specific (Example: There's _a_ new restaurant.)
infinitive	the main form of a verb, usually used with _to_ (Example: I like _to run_ fast.)
informal	friendly or casual language (Example: _Can_ I have that?)
irregular verb	a verb different from regular form verbs (Example: be = _am, are, is, was, were, being_)
modal auxiliary	a verb that indicates a mood (ability, possibility, etc.) and is followed by the base form of another verb (Example: I _can read_ English well.)
modifier	a word phrase that describes another (Example: a _good_ friend)
negative	the opposite of affirmative (Example: She _does not_ like meat.)
noun	a name of a person, place, or thing (Example: _Joe, England, bottle_)
noncount nouns	nouns impossible or difficult to count (Example: _water, love, rice, fire_)

object, direct	the focus of a verb's action (Example: I eat _oranges_.)
object pronoun	replaces the noun taking the action (Example: _Julia_ is nice. I like _her_.)
past tense	a verb form used to express an action or state in the past (Example: You _worked_ yesterday.)
period	a punctuation mark ending a sentence (.)
plural	indicating more than one (Example: _pencils_, _children_)
possessive adjective	an adjective expressing possession (Example: _our_ car)
preposition	a word that indicates relationship between objects (Example: _on_ the _desk_)
present tense	a verb tense representing the current time, not past or future (Example: They _are_ at home right now.)
pronoun	a word used in place of a noun (Example: _Ted_ is 65. _He_ is retired.)
question form	to ask or look for an answer (Example: _Where is my book?_)
regular verb	verb with endings that are regular and follow the rule (Example: work = _work, works, worked, working_)
sentence	a thought expressed in words, with a subject and verb (Example: _Julia works hard._)
short answer	a response to a _yes/no_ question, usually a subject pronoun and auxiliary verb (Example: _Yes, I am_, or _No, he doesn't_.)
singular	one object (Example: _a cat_)
statement	a sentence or thought (Example: _The weather is rainy today_.)
subject	the noun that does the action in a sentence (Example: _The gardener works_ here.)
subject pronoun	a pronoun that takes the place of a subject (Example: _John_ is a sudent. _He_ is smart.)
syllable	a part of a word as determined by vowel sounds and rhythm (Example: _ta-ble_)
tag questions	short informal questions that come at the end of sentences in speech (Example: You like soup, _don't you?_ They aren't hungry, _are they?_)
tense	the part of a verb that shows the past, present, or future time (Example: He _talked_.)
verb	word describing an action or state (Example: The boys _walk_ to school. I _am_ tired.)
vowels	the letters _a, e, i o, u,_ and sometimes _y_
_**wh-**_ **questions**	questions that ask for information, usually starting with _Who, What, When, Where,_ or _Why_. (Example: _Where_ do you live?) _How_ is often included in this group.
**yes/no** **questions**	questions that ask for an affirmative or a negative answer (Example: _Are you happy?_)

GRAMMAR REFERENCE

Subject Pronouns			
Subject pronoun	*Be*	**Information**	**Example sentence**
I	am	a student the teacher Roberto Jasmin a friend	I am a student. *(I'm a student.)*
You	are		You are the teacher.
He	is		He is Roberto.
She			She is Jasmin.
			She is a friend.
You	are	students teachers friends	You are students.
We			We are teachers.
They			They are friends.

Subject pronouns	Possessive adjectives
I am Amal Jahshan.	**My** first name is Amal.
You are a student.	**Your** first name is Amal.
He is a teacher.	**His** address is 25 Fin Road.
She is a student.	**Her** last name is Kusmin.
We are married.	**Our** address is 34 Walker Avenue.
They are married.	**Their** last name is Ramirez.

Simple Present: *Be*			
Affirmative *(yes)*			
Subject	***Be***	**Information**	**Example sentence**
I	am	hungry thirsty	I **am** hungry. *(I'm hungry.)*
He She	is		He **is** hungry. *(He's hungry.)* She **is** hungry. *(She's hungry.)*
We You They	are		We **are** hungry. *(We're hungry.)* You **are** hungry. *(You're hungry.)* They **are** hungry. *(They're hungry.)*
Negative *(no)*			
Subject	***Be***	**Information**	**Example sentence**
I	am not	hungry thirsty	I **am not** hungry. *(I'm not hungry.)*
He She	is not		He **is not** hungry. *(He's not hungry.)* She **is not** hungry. *(She's not hungry.)*
We You They	are not		We **are not** hungry. *(We're not hungry.)* You **are not** hungry. *(You're not hungry.)* They **are not** hungry. *(They're not hungry.)*

Simple Present (Regular)		
Subject	**Verb**	**Example sentence**
I, You, We, They	**see** **visit**	I **see** the doctor once a year. We **visit** the doctor once a year.
He, She, It	**sees** **visits**	He **sees** the doctor once a week. She **visits** the doctor once a week.

Simple Present (Irregular)		
Subject	***Be***	**Example sentence**
I	**am**	I **am** sick.
You, We, They	**are**	We **are** sick.
He, She, It	**is**	He **is** sick.

Simple Present (Irregular)

Subject	*Have*	Example sentence
I, You, We, They	**have**	I **have** a headache.
He, She, It	**has**	She **has** a runny nose.

Simple Present: *Need/Have*

Subject	Verb		Example sentence
I, You, We, They	have	a headache	I have a headache.
	need	aspirin	They need aspirin.
He, She, It	has	a stomachache	He has a stomachache.
	needs	antacid	She needs antacid.
Combinations:	She has a headache. She needs aspirin. You have a stomachache. You need antacid. They have coughs. They need cough syrup.		

Present Continuous

Subject	*Be*	Base + *ing*	Example sentence
I	am	talking	I **am talking**.
He, She, It	is	sleeping	He **is sleeping**.
We, You, They	are	waiting	They **are waiting**.

Simple Past (regular)

Subject	Verb		Example sentence
I, You, He, She, It, We, They	answered	the phones	He answered the phones.
	scheduled	meetings	They scheduled meetings.
	cleaned	the office	We cleaned the office.
	filed	letters	You filed letters.
	smoked	a cigarette	She smoked a cigarette.
	talked	to customers	I talked to customers.
	delivered	packages	She delivered packages.
	helped	customers	We helped customers.

Simple Past (Irregular)			
Subject	**Verb**		**Example sentence**
I, You, He, She, It, We, They	ate (eat)	in the office	She **ate** in the office.
	had (have)	a job	I **had** a job.
	went (go)	to work	We **went** to work.
	saw (see)	a message	She **saw** a message.

Imperative			
Subject	**Verb**		**Example sentence**
~~You~~	wash	your hands	Wash your hands.
	answer	the phones	Answer the phones.
	send	the memos	Send the memos.

Negative Imperative				
Subject	**Verb**			**Example sentence**
~~You~~	don't	make	schedules	Don't make schedules.
		answer	the phones	Don't answer the phones.
		send	the memos	Don't send the memos.

Modal: *Should* (advice)			
Subject	***Should***	**Verb**	**Example sentence**
I, You, He, She, It, We, They	should	take	I **should** take cough syrup.
		go to	You **should** go to the doctor.
		see	He **should** see a doctor.
		sleep	They **should** sleep eight hours.
		make	We **should** make an appointment.

Future: *Will* (goals)

Subject	will	Verb	Example sentence
I, You, He, She, It, We, They	will	exercise	I **will** exercise 30 minutes a day.
		go to	You **will** go to the doctor.
		see	He **will** see a doctor.
		sleep	They **will** sleep eight hours.
		eat	We **will** eat three good meals a day.
Negative			
I, You, He, She, It, We, They	will not	smoke	I **will not** smoke.

Modal: *Can / Can't*

Subject	Can	Verb (base)	Example sentence
I, You, He, She, It, We, They	can	type	I can type.
		mop	He can mop floors.
Subject	**Can't**	**Verb (base)**	**Example sentence**
I, You, He, She, It, We, They	can't	type	I can't type.
		mop	He can't mop floors.

Modal: *May*

Subject	*May* (maybe)	Verb (base)	Example sentence
I, You, He, She, It, We, They	may	help	I may help other students.
		work	He may work on Saturday.

Like + Infinitive

Subject	Verb	Infinitive verb	Example sentence
I, You, We, They	like	to study to work to go to school (work) to eat breakfast (lunch, dinner) to play soccer to talk on the phone	I **like to study**. We **like to eat** lunch at 2:00. They **like to go** to school on Saturday. You **like to work** every day.
He, She, It	likes		He **likes to study** at 1:00. She **likes to work** on Saturday. She **likes to go** to school. He **likes to eat** lunch at 1:00.

Information Questions

Question word	Type of answer	Example question	Answer
What	information (receptionist)	What do you do?	I am a receptionist.
Where	a place (Johnson Company)	Where do you work?	Johnson Company
When	a time or day (9–6) (Monday–Friday)	When do you work?	on Monday at 5:00
Who	a person (Martin)	Who is your teacher?	Mr. Smith

What's and Contractions

Questions

Question word	Verb	Information	Example sentence
What	is	the date today your date of birth your birthplace your first name your last name your address	What is the date today? *(What's the date today?)* What is your date of birth? *(What's your date of birth?)* What is your birthplace? *(What's your birthplace?)* What is your first name? *(What's your first name?)* What is your last name? *(What's your last name?)* What is your address? *(What's your address?)*

Answers

Subject	Verb	Information	Example sentence
The date today	is	September 1st, 2017	The date is September 1st, 2017. *(It's September 1st, 2017.)*
My date of birth		May 13th, 1965	My date of birth is May 13th, 1965. *(It's May 13th, 1965.)*
My birthplace		Mexico	My birthplace is Mexico. *(It's Mexico.)*
My first name		Maria	My first name is Maria. *(It's Maria.)*
My last name		Rodriguez	My last name is Rodriguez. *(It's Rodriguez.)*
My address		2341 First Street	My address is 2341 First St. *(It's 2341 First St.)*

Questions with *How* and *When*

Questions

Question word	Verb	Information	Example sentence
When	is	English class work	When is English class? *(When's English class?)* When is work? *(When's work?)*
How		the weather English class Alex	How is the weather? *(How's the weather?)* How is English class? *(How's English class?)* How is Alex? *(How's Alex?)*

Answers

Subject	Verb	Information	Example sentence
English class	is	at 5:00	English class is at 5:00. *(It's at 5:00.)*
work		at 3:00	Work is at 3:00. *(It's at 3:00.)*
the weather		hot	The weather is hot. *(It's hot.)*
English class		very good	English class is very good. *(It's very good.)*
Alex		fine	Alex is fine.

How much, How many

Questions

Question word		Verb	Information	Example sentence
How much	(money)	is	the blouse	How much is the blouse?
		are	the blouses	How much are the blouses?

Question word		Question structure	Example sentence
How many	blouses	do you want	How many blouses do you want?

Answers

Subject	Verb	Information	Example sentence
the blouse	is	$22.00	The blouse is $22.00. *(It's $22.00.)*
the blouses	are	$20.00	The blouses are $20.00. *(They're $20.00.)*
I	want	three blouses	I want three blouses.

Count Nouns

Questions	Answers
How many shirts are there?	There are two shirts.
How many radios are there?	There is one radio.
How many apples are there?	There are three apples.
How many computers are there?	There is one computer.

Noncount Nouns

Questions	Answers
How much spaghetti is there?	There is one package of spaghetti.
How much water is there?	There are three bottles of water.
How much sugar is there?	There is one bag of sugar.
How much milk is there?	There are two bottles of milk.

Plurals (Spelling)

Regular add -s		Add -es		Exceptions	
Singular	Plural	Singular	Plural	Singular	Plural
jar	jars	sandwich	sandwiches	potato	potatoes
can	cans	bunch	bunches	tomato	tomatoes
bag	bags	radish	radishes		
pound	pounds	box	boxes		
carrot	carrots				
apple	apples				
orange	oranges				

There is, There are	
Singular *(is)*	**Plural**
There **is** one green shirt.	There **are** two black shirts.
There **is** one red pair of shoes.	There **are** two pairs of shoes.
There **is** one blouse in the store.	There **are** three blouses in the store.

Articles *a, an*		
Article **(a=one); (an=one)**	**Singular nouns**	**Example sentence**
	Begin with consonant	
a	carrot	I want **a** carrot.
a	tomato	He wants **a** tomato.
a	pie	They want **a** pie.
	Begin with vowel	
an	**a**pple	I want **an** apple.
an	**e**gg	We need **an** egg.
	Noncount	
	milk	She likes milk.
	water	You drink water.
	sour cream	He adds sour cream.
	cheese	We like cheese.

The		
Noun		**Example sentence**
the	house car store	I live in the house on First Street. We take the bus. They go to the store.
Proper noun		**Example sentence**
~~the~~	Shoe Emporium Polly's Pets Clothes Mart	Shoe Emporium is on City Mall Drive. Polly's Pets is next to American Bank. Clothes Mart is in back of the bank.

Prepositions

a. It's **in the front of** the store.	
b. It's **in the corner of** the store.	
c. It's **in the middle of** the store.	
d. It's **in the back of** the store.	
e. It's **on the left side of** the store.	
f. It's **on the right side of** the store.	

Prepositions of Location

Preposition		Example sentence
in		The tuna fish is **in** the canned goods section.
on		The green beans are **on** the top shelf.
over		The corn is **over** the tomato sauce.
between		The tomato sauce is **between** the pears and the tuna fish.
next to		The peas are **next to** the corn.

PHOTO CREDITS

03 (tl) Andresr/Shutterstock.com, (tr) StockLite/Shutterstock.com, (cl) Mel Yates/Digital Vision/Getty Images, (cr) Dmitry Kalinovsky/Shutterstock.com, 04 (tl) Fotoluminate LLC/Shutterstock.com, (tc1) Photos.com, (tc2) © IndexOpen, (tr) ImageSource/SuperStock, 05 (cl) Baerbel Schmidt/Getty Images, (cr) StockLite/Shutterstock.com, 09 (t) Africa Studio/Shutterstock.com, (c) photastic/Shutterstock.com, (b) Wavebreakmedia/Shutterstock.com, 12 (tl) Andrey Orletsky/Shutterstock.com, (tc1) Myrleen Ferguson Cate/PhotoEdit, (tc2) Amy Eckert/UpperCut Images/Getty Images, (tr) Spencer Grant/PhotoEdit, 18 (t) Oliver Eltinger/Fancy/Corbis, (c) VStock/Alamy, (b) Fiona Conrad/Crave/Corbis, 20 (cl) Kevin Peterson/Photodisc/Getty Images, (c1), (c2) © Hemera Photodisc, (cr) Amy Eckert/UpperCut Images/Getty Images,, 21 Beboy/Shutterstock.com, 28 (tl) Andresr/Shutterstock.com, (tc1) StockLite/Shutterstock.com, (tc2) Mel Yates/Digital Vision/Getty Images, (tr) Dmitry Kalinovsky/Shutterstock.com, 31 (tl) Africa Studio/Shutterstock.com, (tc) Jason/Alamy, 34 (tl) Africa Studio/Shutterstock.com, (tc) Warwick Lister-Kaye/Getty Images, (tr) Early Spring/Shutterstock.com, (cl) naipung/Shutterstock.com, (c), (cr) Photos.com, (bl) Wavebreakmedia/Shutterstock.com, (bc) Jason/Alamy, 40 (tl), (cr) Photos.com, (tc1), (c2) Peshkova/

Shutterstock.com, (tc2) S_Photo/Shutterstock.com, (tr) sirirak kaewgorn/Shutterstock.com, (cl) PhotoObjects/RF/Getty Images, (c1) Paul Tearle/Getty Images, 41 (tl), (tc2) Photos.com, (tc1) sirirak kaewgorn/Shutterstock.com, (tr) Paul Tearle/Getty Images, (cl) Peshkova/Shutterstock.com, (c) fototi photography/Shutterstock.com, (cr) D. Hurst/Alamy, 44 (t1) Mmkarabella/Shutterstock.com, (t2) K2 PhotoStudio/Shutterstock.com, (c) Grisha Bruev/Shutterstock.com, (b1) Candus Camera/Shutterstock.com, (b2) Kati Molin/Shutterstock.com, 47 (tl) J Shepherd/Ocean/Corbis, (tc) Harry Bischof/Getty Images, (tr) Ildi Papp/Shutterstock.com, (cl) NatashaPhoto/Shutterstock.com, (c) Foodio/Shutterstock.com, (cr) Ian O'Leary/Getty Images, 50 (tl) Christian Draghici/Shutterstock.com, (tc) Pack/Shutterstock.com, (tr) Guzel Studio/Shutterstock.com, (cl) Burke/Triolo Productions/FoodPix/Jupiterimages, (c) Andersen Ross/Photodisc/Getty Images, 52 (tl) (tr) (cl) (cr2) Photos.com, (cr1) IndexOpen, 56 (tl) Candus Camera/Shutterstock.com, (tc) Amarita/Shutterstock.com, (tr) Burke/Triolo Productions/FoodPix/Jupiterimages, (cl) Christian Draghici/Shutterstock.com, (c) Photos.com, (cr) HandmadePictures/Shutterstock.com, (bl) Ozgur Coskun/Shutterstock.com, (bc) Brent Hofacker/

Shutterstock.com, 76 (tl) (cl1) fiphoto/Shutterstock.com, (cl2) Mangostock/Shutterstock.com, (bl) Niki Love/Shutterstock.com, 82 (t) zentilia/Shutterstock.com, (c1) luckyraccoon/Shutterstock.com, (c2) kristian sekulic/Getty Images, (b) after6pm/Sutterstock.com, 84 (t) Maridav/Shutterstock.com, (c) light poet/Shutterstock.com, (b) kristian sekulic/Getty Images, 85 (t) kristian sekulic/Getty Images, (c) Maridav/Shutterstock.com, (b) light poet/Shutterstock.com, 92 Brooke Whatnall/National Geographic Creative, 93 (t) Photos.com/RF (c) Imageworks/Getty Images, 95 (cl) Gpointstudio/Shutterstock.com, (c) Photographee.eu/Shutterstock.com, (cr) Stefano Cavoretto/Shutterstock.com, 99 (tl) Gpointstudio/Shutterstock.com, (tc) Alexander Raths/Shutterstock.com, (tr) Maskot/Getty Images, 102 (tl) Amos Morgan/Photodisc/Getty Images, (tc) blvdone/Shutterstock.com, (tr) lzf/Shutterstock.com, 108 (tr) Helen King/Comet/Corbis, (cr) auremar/Shutterstock.com, 111 (t) auremar/Shutterstock.com, 123 Elena Elisseeva/Shutterstock.com, 124 (tl) Mark Anderson/Rubberball/Alamy, (tc) Amy Eckert/UpperCut Images/Getty Images, (tr) Edhar/Shutterstock.com, (cl) StockLite/Shutterstock.com, (c) Mel Yates/Digital Vision/Getty Images, (cr) Andresr/Shutterstock.com, 125 Inspiron.Dell.Vector/Shutterstock.com.

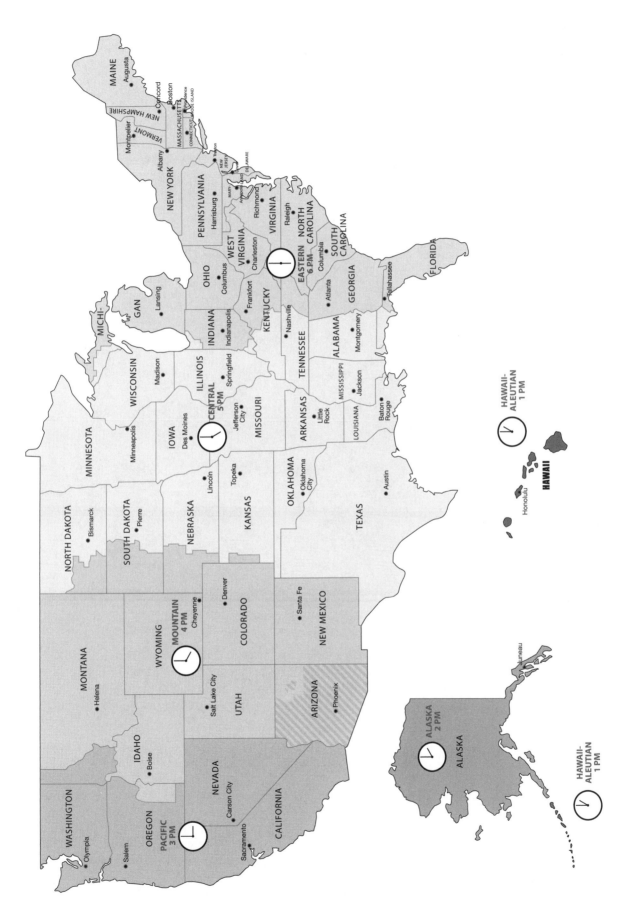